Christian Holiness

in Scripture,
in History,
and in Life

Christian Holiness

in Scripture, in History, and in Life

by

George Allen Turner

Beacon Hill Press of Kansas City
Kansas City, Missouri

Copyright, 1977
Beacon Hill Press of Kansas City

ISBN: 0-8341-0463-6

Printed in the
United States of America

Contents

Preface

Ours is a less tranquil, less meditative age than most previous ones. However, the temper of the times is introspective, questioning. Many are seeking for meaning and values. The Scriptures remain our surest Guide to truth and reality in such spiritual values. The relevancy of these biblical truths was never more obvious or more needful than today.

These essays on the doctrine of biblical holiness, especially in the Wesleyan tradition, were given in several institutions. They are here presented essentially as delivered orally. The audiences were mostly college students, graduate students in theology, and clergymen. The essays are presented, however, in a popular style with a minimum of technical terms and documentation. These messages aim not at a rethinking or restructuring of biblical doctrines, or of Wesleyan thought. Instead they seek to clarify and articulate the essentials and to note their relevance in the last half of the 20th century.

Special appreciation is due to the president and faculty of Nazarene Theological Seminary for the invitation to deliver the Gould Lectures on biblical theology. My thanks also for similar invitations and courtesies from Osaka Christian College, Japan; Holy Light Theological College, Taiwan; the Union Biblical Seminaries in India and in Colombia; the South India Bible Institute; the Free Methodist faculty in Sao Paulo, Brazil; and Trevecca Nazarene College in Nashville, Tenn.

Publication is prompted by a desire to make these messages available to a wider public. Appreciation is due the publisher for making this possible. It is hoped that the printed word will meet with as cordial a response as the oral delivery. The call to holy living is not only the greatest of privileges, but also a challenge that cannot lightly be dismissed.

—GEORGE ALLEN TURNER

Chapter 1

The Message of Holiness in the Bible

The quest for Christlike living, voiced so powerfully in the New Testament, and occasionally emphasized during subsequent centuries, especially in the ministry of John and Charles Wesley, is a continuing movement. Those who stress holy living number several million, some in churches featuring this doctrine, thousands of others in the "popular" churches. Most of us are interested in the Wesleyan message only to the extent that it represents God's revelation to man, only to the extent that it represents the teaching of the New Testament.

A. ESSENTIALS OF THE MESSAGE

What are the essentials of this New Testament message as interpreted by Wesley and others? These essentials include:

1. *The assurance that one's sins are forgiven.* This is the significance of John Wesley's experience at Aldersgate. It was there, for the first time, he knew that his own sins were forgiven, and that Christ was his personal Saviour. Though he had been a religious man of great earnestness for many years, this, he says, was the first time that personal assurance was given concerning his relationship to his Lord.

2. *The fellowship of those who are "born anew."* The institution that testified to the importance of fellowship was the Methodist class meeting. Patterned after the fellowship of believers at Herrnhut, Germany, the early Methodists gathered in groups of 12 under a leader to lay bare their souls to each other and to God. This fellowship was the nucleus of the people called Methodists.

3. *The use of the means of grace.* This was the issue upon which Wesley parted company with many others whose Christian experience he recognized and whose fellowship he cherished. Wesley and his followers insisted that means of grace were not "works of the flesh," but rather channels by which the grace of God normally operates.[1] Thus they avoided what they felt to be the snare of lawlessness or antinomianism, the delusion that faith without works is sufficient.

4. *Witnessing.* The sharing of the message received an emphasis seldom given since the first century. The evangelicals of the 18th century witnessed in homes, on the street, in the shop—everywhere. This led Wesley to proclaim, "The world is my parish."

5. *The quest for holiness.* This dominates the concern of John Wesley from the age of 25 years until the age of 38 when he found the way of faith; henceforth, he was its chief witness and exponent.

6. *Loving God supremely.* What does holiness involve? When called before the Anglican bishop of London to defend his "heretical" views, Wesley insisted that his main emphasis was upon loving God with all the heart, soul, and strength, and one's neighbor as oneself. This, Wesley correctly concluded, is pleasing to all men. Who can object to love? Probably the hymn that best describes the genius of the Methodist revival is one included in nearly all hymnals and which ranks among the 10 greatest hymns.

> *Love divine, all loves excelling,*
> *Joy of heaven, to earth come down;*
> *Fix in us Thy humble dwelling,*
> *All Thy faithful mercies crown!*
> —CHARLES WESLEY

While to Luther God appeared primarily as *Judge* and to Calvin primarily as *Ruler*, Wesley was impressed most of all by the *love* of God.[2] He was saved from a cheap sentimentalism by an equal awareness of the holiness of God. This meant that the

---

1. John R. Parris, *John Wesley's Doctrine of the Sacraments* (London: Epworth Press, 1963), p. 97.
2. See this theme pursued convincingly in Mildred Bangs Wynkoop, *A Theology of Love* (Kansas City: Beacon Hill Press of Kansas City, 1972).

one who professed to love God must at the same time live a righteous life. Wesley often affirmed that holiness also meant "having the mind of Christ and walking as Christ walked." It is the Christ-centered life.

7. *Holy living also called for doctrinal clarity.* While theirs was not primarily a theological movement, the early Methodist leaders were concerned with sound doctrine. On occasion the Wesleys could contend for the faith with great effectiveness, and often did so. Among the best evidences of John's skill as a polemical theologian was his discourse on "Original Sin" addressed to a forceful contemporary advocate of a Pelagian position.[3]

8. *Social service was another element in the Wesleyan definition of holy living.* Members of the "Holy Club" at Oxford, long before "Aldersgate," made it their business not only to go to church but also to the jails, to the streets, to the poor. They were activists in the best sense of the term. Evidence for this social concern is seen again in the class meeting, where one of the chief responsibilities of the class leader was to receive offerings for the poor.

In one of their earliest statements of self-consciousness, the Methodists said their task was to "reform the nation and to spread scriptural holiness throughout the lands." They were not recluses, isolating themselves from the world in quest for a better life; they were practical. In a sense they were mystics, concerned primarily with pleasing God but recognizing that this called also for bearing witness by word and deed to their contemporaries. From the perspective of two centuries it is obvious that the early Methodists were concerned not only with pulling brands from the burning but also in putting out the fire.[4] They were interested in getting at the root of evils as well as dealing with the fruits.

B. OLD TESTAMENT ROOTS OF THE MESSAGE

He who pursues the biblical doctrine of the holy life in the Old Testament is likely to be frustrated more than once. Most

---

3. This treatise on "Original Sin" was an answer to Rev. Taylor's thoughtful essay on the subject.
4. W. E. Sangster criticized the early Methodists at this point (*The Path to Perfection*, pp. 194 ff.).

popular treatments of the subject are weak in exegesis. Many exponents are earnest, evangelical, and correct in doctrine, but they are not skilled in the technical tools necessary for biblical exegesis, especially in Semitic languages. The result is that many works otherwise commendable for doctrine and persuasiveness are weak and sometimes erroneous in exegesis.

On the other hand, books that deal with the subject of holiness in the Old Testament on exegetical grounds are, for the most part, unsatisfactory theologically. Usually they are by critical or liberal scholars who do not bring to their task a complete confidence in the integrity and trustworthiness of the Scriptures. Many of these scholars have been influenced by theological presuppositions that make them indifferent to the spiritual insights of the biblical authors.

1. God's Holiness

The conviction that God is both holy and righteous is one of the most distinctive features of the Old Testament. A glance at a concordance indicates that no major doctrine is more important than holiness. The prominence of the theme is seen in the fact that words translated *holiness* and *sanctification* appear more than 800 times.

What are the essential features of the Old Testament doctrine of God's holiness? The careful student will soon discover that holiness is not just one of several attributes of God; it is rather a part of His essential nature. Holiness is the central nature of the being of God from which such attributes as love, justice, and mercy emanate. Therefore, no one can concern himself for any length of time with biblical thought without confronting the challenge of holiness.

Such a recognition is an important corrective for the idea which is current now that if God is still alive, He is pretty well humanized. Some apparently think of God as a good-natured genie who can be summoned at will to help us in our tasks or to fulfill our aspirations. Others consider Him too remote to be involved, too distant to respond to the requests of finite beings. They disparage intercession, believing that prayer changes only the petitioner, not the outcome. Others, like Job's self-appointed counsellors, consider God's holiness so austere and distant that holiness in man is impossible, and that aspirations after it are therefore presumptuous.

God's holiness includes not only brilliance and separateness; His holiness also includes righteousness. It is difficult for us, after these centuries of Judeo-Christian tradition, to think of any god as other than righteous. It is a fact, however, that the gods of even the most sophisticated pagans were usually amoral beings; they were "gods" with whom righteousness was not linked. This makes more conspicuous by contrast the Hebrew insistence that the God they worshipped is entirely righteous. His righteousness is seen in the fact that when God's own people sinned, He rejected and disciplined them. Even the holy ark and the holy sanctuary were not spared when righteousness ceased to be associated with them. The biblical teaching is that sanctity is more important than survival; paradoxically, the "system" had to be destroyed by the Exile in order to save it through the Remnant.

God reveals himself not only in words but by deeds. His words made it crystal clear: "Ye shall be holy, for I the Lord your God am holy" (Lev. 19:2). His actions were equally clear, as when He forsook the people in the wilderness when they sinned, compelling them to seek Him outside the camp (Exodus 32—34). Jerusalem was given to understand that although she was called the Holy City, yet if sin were found there, God would repudiate the Temple, the city, and the people, bringing all of them under judgment (Isaiah 4; Jeremiah 7). Historical Jerusalem was destroyed in 587-586 B.C. in order to salvage the Holy City.

The revelation of God's holiness makes a clear exposure of *man's sinfulness*. It was only after Isaiah "saw the Lord . . . high and lifted up" and heard the attendants before the throne crying, "Holy, holy, holy," that he saw his own inward corruption (Isaiah 6:1-4). The man described in the seventh chapter of Romans came to recognize his own sinfulness only after being confronted by the righteousness of the law. So holiness exposes its opposite, sin. It is often said, by way of generalization, that in the Old Testament, sin is largely corporate guilt and limited to overt acts. However, there is also much there to indicate concern with the perversity of one's heart. This comes into clear focus in Genesis, where God was concerned with the "evil . . . imagination" which pervaded mankind (Gen. 6:1-6). It comes to most emphatic expression in the later prophets, especially in Jeremiah who was impressed

11

and oppressed by man's chronic perversity; his tendency to evil (Jer. 3:13, 17, 21). A study of several synonyms for "hardness of heart," "crookedness," "perversity," and the like, reveals a significant facet of Old Testament theology; in the Old Testament itself there is a recognition of a *source* of sin lying behind the *acts* of sin. Man's major problem, "heart trouble," will be cured by the implantation of a "new heart" (Ezek. 36:25-27).

2. God Calls to Holy Living

The conviction that God is holy has as its corollary the persuasion that God's people should be like Him in holiness. Because separation is a main ingredient in the biblical doctrine of holiness, God calls for separation. From what were the Israelites to be separated? They were to keep themselves separate from other nations, especially those peoples who would lead them astray. They were to be free from sin. They were to be separated unto God, a peculiar people, a holy nation (Deut. 7:1-10). They were not to be separated, however, just for the sake of separation. The separation was only the means to an end. This end was to be righteous, to be like God. Separation did not mean being peculiar in the sense of being queer. It did mean, however, that in order to be loyal to God, they would have to be distinctive. There is no holiness apart from separation. This separation is twofold: separation from that which is common or unclean, and dedication to God and to God's exclusive service. Thus the Israelites were designated as unique: a kingdom of priests, a holy nation (Exod. 19:6; Deut. 7:6; 1 Pet. 2:9).

3. Perfection in Righteousness

What does it mean to be "perfect"? In biblical language the term is not one that can be safely avoided, because it is prominent in both Old and New Testaments. It is important in communicating this truth to recognize that the biblical concept of "perfect" is not that of "flawlessness," which is the contemporary English meaning. Nor is it to be watered down to include deviations from the norm or the ideal. It means, rather, a relative perfection. Among those so designated were Noah, Abraham, and Job.

As an analogy we may recall that certain individuals in history are called "the Great," such as Alexander the Great, Herod the Great, and Peter the Great of Russia. The characterization of a person as "the Great" is not only to distinguish him from other individuals of the same name, but also to indicate that he was greater than others. In a similar manner certain Old Testament characters were called "perfect" or "just." Their perfection was relative. They were "perfect" by comparison with their contemporaries. They were outstanding and conspicuous for piety, integrity, and righteousness. They were, in fact, like God, with reference to goodness. Enoch, Noah, Abraham, Moses, David, and Job were thus honored.

To be perfect meant specifically to be without blemish (cf. Deut. 18:13), not faultless, but blameless. Therefore most newer versions of the Scripture avoid the term "perfect," as applied to persons, and use "blameless" instead (e.g., Gen. 17:1, RSV). The word used is the same as that applied to animals which were fit for presentation to God (Exod. 12:5). These animals were not maimed or crippled; they were physically sound and whole. In like manner, the person who is perfect, in the Old Testament sense of the term, is one who is wholehearted, unswerving, and undivided in his allegiance to God. He is conspicuous for righteousness.

Any layman can distinguish a casual, nominal Christian from a dedicated disciple. As a Moslem guide once put it, "There are Moslems, and then there are real Moslems." The same can be said of Christians. Halford Luccock once said, "When a Christian goes Christian, that makes news." None of the ancient Hebrews were perfect in the sense that they were without flaw. Many of them, however, were perfect in terms of integrity and loyalty—a perfection in love, a perfection of the heart. Among the best examples of these men who were both great and good are Joseph, Samuel, and Daniel, about whom no sinful acts or attitudes are recorded.

C. From the Old Covenant to the New

In the Old Testament the Spirit of God came only upon certain individuals in times of national crisis. The Spirit-filled men were mostly the prophets. Some of the kings were anointed by the Spirit, but the term "Holy Spirit" occurs only three times in the entire Old Testament (Ps. 51:11; Isa. 63:10-11). The Spirit represents the "breath" of God (e.g., Gen. 2:7; Ezek. 37:5; John 3:8). He is the Person of the Godhead in closest relationship to man. This truth is reflected in the Genesis account of creation when it says, not only that God's Spirit moved over the face of the deep, but also that God breathed into man's nostrils the "breath of life." The word for "spirit," "breath," and "wind" is the same in Hebrew *(ruach)*.

The Spirit of God in the Old Testament not only inspired sacred speech, as in the case of the prophets, but He also inspired national leaders in times of crisis. God's Spirit is pictured as giving life to the land and to its people (Isa. 44:3-4; Ezek. 36:25-27). The promise of still better times to come is reflected in Joel, Ezekiel, and elsewhere. Here the distinctive feature of the new covenant, in contrast to the old, is the greater liberality with which God bestows His Spirit upon the common people: both men and women, servants and handmaids, bondmen and free men (Joel 2:29). The new covenant is more democratic, it reaches more people, it comes closer to the objective of biblical redemption: namely, God and man at one— the atonement. It was in the sixth century before Christ, a century of major crises, that the greatest prominence is given to the doctrine of the Spirit of God.[5]

During the intertestament period there was greater stress upon God's transcendence, less upon His immanence. Consistent with this was emphasis upon revelation through angels and less on revelation by the Spirit. Indeed, it was believed because of the sins of the people that God's personal presence, the *shekinah,* had withdrawn from the Temple, the city, and the people (cf. Ezek. 10:4, 18; 11:23) into the "seventh heaven," there to remain until the days of the Messiah.

An interesting exception to the neglect of the doctrine of the Spirit is the literature of the Qumran community near the Dead Sea. Here, especially in their hymns and in their *Manual of Discipline,* the Holy Spirit is mentioned as purifying the mind and the heart. However, it is a purification in which no distinction is made between ritual and morals.[6] The interesting

5. See I. F. Wood, *The Spirit of God in Biblical Literature* (New York: Armstrong and Son, 1904), p. 52.
6. T. H. Gaster, trans., *The Dead Sea Scriptures* (New York: Doubleday and Co., 1964), p. 50-55.

14

thing is, however, that cleansing is linked with the ministry of the Spirit as prominently as it is in either the Old or New Testament. In the hymns of the Qumran community the emphasis upon the Spirit indicates that the writers were, in a sense, mystics, stressing as they did the immediate contact between God and the believer.

D. THE MESSAGE IN THE NEW TESTAMENT

The witness of the New Testament to the possibility of living a holy life in this world is extensive, and a proper interpretation of it must begin with an understanding of what sanctification is, or the kinds of sanctification referred to. This treatment will be somewhat cursory and will seek only to set things in perspective, rather than to engage in depth with this important subject.

1. Positional Sanctification

Positional sanctification refers both to things and to people. That things may be sanctified is illustrated in the text "The altar that sanctifieth the gift" (Matt. 23:19). This is sanctification in the sense that offerings placed upon the sacred altar no longer belong to the donor but to God. It is a sanctification by association, an "imputed" righteousness. This sanctification may be the result of mere physical contact or of proximity.

The same concept applies to persons. It is in this sense in the Old Testament that Aaron and his sons were "sanctified" for the work of the priesthood. Today when a layman becomes an ordained minister of the gospel, he has an imputed holiness which he did not have before. He is now engaged in a sacred calling. He is separated from other men and has committed himself to serve the Lord exclusively. Because of his being set apart from secular pursuits and dedicated to God's service, there is a sense in which he is a holy man professionally. He may not be any more intrinsically holy than before; his character may remain the same. There is no actual moral difference conferred by any "imputed" righteousness. It may be in this sense of committing himself to a task that Jesus said, "I sanctify myself, that they also might be sanctified through the truth." And in this sense, at least, Jesus prayed that His

15

disciples might be "sanctified through the truth" (John 17:17-19; cf. 10:36).

2. Initial Sanctification

Those who differ from the Wesleyan interpretation of the holy life and its possibilities do so with special reference to the matter of entire sanctification. Most biblical scholars will agree that sanctification is taught in the New Testament as being the privilege of every believer, but not all attach the same meaning to this term. When Paul wrote to the church at Rome and to the church at Corinth, he greeted all of them as those who are "sanctified in Christ Jesus, called to be saints" (1 Cor. 1:2; cf. Rom. 1:7). This is what may be termed as initial sanctification. It is sanctification which recognizes that separation from the world and commitment to God are prerequisites of being a Christian.

In writing of conversion, Wiley speaks of "initial" sanctification:

> Defilement attaches to sinful acts, and so also does guilt, which is the consciousness of sin as our own. There must be, therefore, this initial cleansing, concomitant with the other blessings of the first work of grace, if this guilt and acquired depravity are to be removed from the sinner.[7]

3. Progressive Sanctification

From another perspective sanctification in the New Testament is said to be progressive. This corresponds to "imparted" righteousness, and it begins at conversion, continuing constantly through the life of the Christian. Every Christian is sanctified in the sense that he becomes a "partaker . . . of the divine nature" (2 Pet. 1:4). His nature is being "renewed" by the Holy Spirit; he has been "regenerated" or "born again." This is the usage that sanctification normally has for writers and speakers in the Reformed tradition. It is the positive side of justification; it has to do with the Spirit of God making actual in the believer the positive renewal of his nature into the likeness of God's nature. This is seen, for example, in such

7. H. Orton Wiley, *Christian Theology* (Kansas City: Nazarene Publishing House, 1941), 2:480-81.

16

texts as Acts 20:32; 26:18; 1 Cor. 6:11; Eph. 5:26; and Heb. 10:14; 13:12.

4. Entire Sanctification

There is general agreement up to this point, but one is in a minority if he goes on to affirm that the New Testament also teaches *entire* sanctification. This is the conviction that God's positive renewal of one's fallen nature can be consummated by faith, instantaneously, prior to death, or as soon as the conditions of commitment and trust are exercised. The process of entire sanctification differs, of course, from that of justification in that it deals, not with the guilt arising from acts in the past, but with a condition of sinfulness which remains even in those who believe. Many are convinced that they have discovered in the Bible, and in experience, this work of full salvation from indwelling defilement. This they are bold enough to acknowledge, not in the sense of an achievement or an attainment, but rather as something obtained as a gift of free grace. It is no more a cause for boasting, or a feeling of superiority, than would be one's conversion by which he is transferred "from the power of darkness, and . . . translated . . . into the kingdom of his dear Son" (Col. 1:13).

Entire sanctification is twofold in nature. Negatively, it calls for separation from sin, as in Rom. 6:1-11, where Paul points out, with great emphasis, that if a Christian is united with Christ in death and resurrection, the sin problem has been decisively defeated, as a result of the work of Christ. "Sin," says Paul triumphantly, "shall not have dominion over you." The same conviction is voiced in passages such as Acts 15:9; 2 Cor. 7:1; and Jas. 4:8.

It is passages such as these, in Pauline writings, which have led a noted German historian, in the liberal tradition of Adolph Harnack, to say, "The victorious warfare against sin, which once took place in Jesus, is repeated anew in every Christian to whom the Spirit has been given. The Spirit seizes control of a man, breaks the power of the passions of the flesh, and levels the road to the life according to God's will."[8] Lietzmann continues, "At the beginning of this process of salvation is the decisive

8. Hans Lietzman, *Beginnings of the Christian Church* (New York: Charles Scribner's Sons, 1937), 1:155-56.

17

work of justification and a new birth of the Spirit in baptism. The Christian is now righteous, dead to sin and freed from its power."[9] German New Testament scholars, such as Windisch and Lietzmann, may not believe that Paul was correct in this, but they do believe this to be Paul's meaning.

There are three important facets of sanctification. One is *recognition of God as uniquely holy* (Matt. 6:9; Luke 11:2; 1 Pet. 3:15). We do this every time we repeat the Lord's Prayer, "Hallowed by thy name." Sanctification also means *dedication or consecration,* as is seen, for example, in John 10:36; 17:19; Rom. 12:1; 15:6; 2 Tim. 2:21. This is something that man can do, and it is a condition upon which God can give purity of heart.

The main facet of the meaning of sanctification is that of *cleansing.* This kind of cleansing is rooted in the Old Testament, especially in Psalm 51. Here is probably the clearest picture to be found in the Old Testament of a man seeking purity of heart. David cries, "Purge me with hyssop, and I shall be clean: wash me, and I shall be whiter than snow" (Ps. 51:7). The verb for cleanse is *katharidzō,* with numerous occurrences. Some refer only to ceremonial cleansing (Matt. 23:26) while many others demand moral cleansing from sin (Acts 15:9; 2 Cor. 7:1; Eph. 5:26; Titus 2:14).

Another word, *hagnidzō,* means to purify. This likewise is used to describe the removal of sin from the heart (Jas. 4:8; 1 Pet. 1:22; 1 John 3:3). The positive emphasis connected with cleansing or purification is expressed in a word usually translated "renew" *(anakainoō).* This is seen, for example, in the "renewing of your mind" called for in the Epistle to the Romans (Rom. 12:2; cf. 2 Cor. 4:16; Col. 3:10; Titus 3:5).

5. Results of Entire Sanctification

1. Godlikeness. In New Testament terminology one result of this work of grace within the heart is spiritual wholeness *(holoklaris).* This experience unifies the whole personality under the Lordship of Jesus and the canopy of love. This can come only when God has us in our entirety. Self-life is yielded to Christ and renewed in His likeness. This change is also spoken of as being recreated in the "image of God." It is Godlikeness.

9. *Ibid.,* p. 159.

We are to be like our Father in heaven, who deals with His enemies better than they deserve (Matt. 5:43-48; Rom. 12:21; cf. Col. 3:10).

b. Christlikeness. Another result of this entire sanctification is having "the mind of Christ." The New Testament writers had the audacity to say that believers could have, while still human, the attitude toward things that Jesus possessed. They could think the way He thinks, have His perspective, have a disposition like His. They could react under crises the way Jesus did (1 Cor. 2:16; Phil. 2:5; Heb. 12:2; 1 Pet. 2:21).

c. Purity. Sanctification means, above everything else, victory over sin. Nowhere does the New Testament tell us that the believer needs to struggle against indwelling sin until he is delivered by death. No provision is made anywhere in the New Testament for the remains of sin to continue; instead, the repeated emphasis is to expect full deliverance through the grace of Christ (Rom. 6:14-22; 8:1-11; Col. 1:22; 1 John 1:9; 3:9).

The New Testament is more emphatic about the *entirety* of the cleansing than specifying it as occurring in two distinct crises. There are passages in which the second crisis is explicit (1 Thess. 3:13; 5:23), and others in which it is implied (2 Cor. 7:1). Still other passages stress the entirety but omit a specific reference to a second crisis.

The sum total of New Testament teachings, however, makes it clear, both explicitly and implicitly, that full deliverance comes normally in two works of grace. One reason is the twofold nature of sin, which needs both pardon for sinful acts and purity for a sinful nature or inclination (cf. Titus 3:5). The teaching of two works of grace is based also upon the recognition of two natures in the regenerate: the Spirit of God and the spirit of "the world" or "the flesh" (Rom. 7:22-23; 8:5-13; Gal. 5:16-25; Jas. 1:8). There is no provision in the New Testament for a tolerance of sin (Rom. 13:14). Instead, full deliverance from sin is envisioned (Rom. 6:1-22; 1 Thess. 5:12-23). Furthermore, there is the apostolic precedent of men being clearly saved (John 17:6) but later, at Pentecost, having had their hearts purified (Acts 15:9). The change in their lives is dramatic evidence of the change in their spirits that occurred at Pentecost.

d. Perfect in Love. The term "perfect love" comes from the

19

First Epistle of John (4:17-18). In this short and trenchant letter, God is said to be the Source of light, truth, and love. It follows that God's children also are characterized by love for the brethren and for others (1 John 3:14). Love is said to be "perfect" or complete when nothing contrary to love remains in the believer. Perfect love links the believer to the Source of love so intimately that he is unafraid of judgment. "As he is, so are we in this world" (1 John 4:17). Perfect love leaves no room for resentments, bitterness, ill will, or malice.

Peter agreed: "Above all hold unfailing your love for one another, since love covers a multitude of sins" (1 Pet. 4:8, RSV). In the famous "ladder of piety" love is located at the top, above all of the other virtues (2 Pet. 1:7).

This love extends not only to friends but embraces enemies as well (Matt. 5:43-48). It is demonstrated by Jesus and Stephen praying for their tormenters (Luke 23:24; Acts 7:60). This type of love *(agapē)* is deliberate and purposeful; it involves choice, is not impulsive, and comes only from God.

e. Spirit-filled. The New Testament is vibrant with special reference to the fulfillment of the Old Testament prophecies concerning the bestowal of God's Spirit upon believing humanity. It tells us that God will bestow His Spirit in His fullness on the receptive believer. The Spirit-filled life is normative for the Christian (Luke 24:44; Acts 1:5, 8; 2:4; Eph. 5:18).

The work of the Spirit is one of the more difficult phases of New Testament theology, not so much because we are ignorant of what God is and wills, but rather because we are so ignorant about who we are and what we are like. It is difficult, for example, to distinguish between the human and the carnal, between our spirit and the divine Spirit resident in believers.

Another difficulty that is particularly prominent now is that of distinguishing between the *gifts* and the *graces* of the Spirit. The New Testament makes it abundantly clear that spiritual gifts are not necessarily an evidence of Christian maturity. These gifts are to be welcomed and recognized as genuine; yet they are no substitute for perfect love. The fruit of the Spirit is far more important in the New Testament than are the gifts, such as prophecy, tongues, and healing (1 Corinthians 12—14).

We must never forget that the times of church renewal through the centuries have been times when the Holy Spirit was sought and welcomed in the daily life of believers. Indeed, the Spirit-possessed life in the New Testament is the norm. No longer is the Spirit-filled person limited to prophets and extraordinary individuals; rather, the Spirit is bestowed generously on all willing, obedient hearts. God still gives His Holy Spirit in fullness to those who obey Him (Acts 5:32). While it is true that all Christians are born of the Spirit, it is also true that not all Christians are consistently filled with the Spirit. Yet this is the Father's choicest gift to His own (Luke 11:13; Acts 2:38). Why are we not more ardently and constantly concerned with the reception and retention of the Father's Gift in His fullness? The person who is healthy spiritually is one who hungers and thirsts for more of God.

> *O come, and dwell in me,*
> *Spirit of power within!*
> *And bring the glorious liberty*
> *From sorrow, fear, and sin.*
>
> *Hasten the joyful day*
> *Which shall my sins consume;*
> *When old things shall be done away,*
> *And all things new become.*
>
> *I want the witness, Lord,*
> *That all I do is right,*
> *According to Thy will and Word,*
> *Well pleasing in Thy sight.*
>
> *I ask no higher state;*
> *Indulge me but in this,*
> *And soon or later then translate*
> *To my eternal bliss.*
>
> —CHARLES WESLEY

Chapter 2

The Message of Holiness in Christian History

The early Methodists, especially the Wesleys, were deeply influenced by the tradition of which they were the heirs. They were influenced not only by the New Testament but by the early Fathers, especially those of the first two centuries. John Wesley acknowledged specific indebtedness to Clement of Alexandria for his portrait of the Christian Gnostic and to John Cassian for his lectures to monks on the holy life. He also expressed his gratitude to men like Thomas a Kempis for his *Imitation of Christ* and to Richard Baxter, Jeremy Taylor, and William Law of the Church of England.

A. The Ancient Witness (A.D. 100-500)

The period following the New Testament was not a time of much literary activity or achievement. But among the early witnesses to Christian perfection was Clement of Rome (fl. A.D. 100), who echoed the thoughts of Paul in urging upon his readers the perfect love which casts out fear. His letter to the Roman church indicates how deeply he was influenced by the New Testament with its assurance of victory over sin.

A longing for the primitive days of miracles and the dynamic activity of the Holy Spirit found expression in Montanus, who called for a return from formality in worship to the days of Pentecost. Unfortunately, he concluded that he himself was an incarnation of the Holy Spirit. But that he was able to have any influence at all testifies to the longing of the

22

church of the mid-second century for the days of power that the Church knew 100 years earlier.

Perhaps the first sermon on Christian perfection was published by Tatian about A.D. 160 in which he expounded the conversation between Jesus and the rich young ruler (Matt. 19:16-30). He was explaining what Jesus meant by perfection with its call to renunciation and ardent discipleship.

Another luminary was Clement of Alexandria (fl. A.D. 200), learned both in the classics and in the gospel. He was unwilling to let the Gnostics take credit beyond their due and therefore boldly announced himself as a "Christian Gnostic." In so doing, he indicated that although knowledge is not antagonistic to the evangel, yet the most important virtue in Christianity is not knowledge—it is love.

Tertullian, a contemporary of Clement, wrote in Latin. He exhorted zealously for separation from the world and for an uncompromising commitment to the demands of the Gospels. Meanwhile the church was faced with two threats to its witness to full salvation. One was the Gnostic heresy in which believers were divided between those who simply "believed" and those who were "perfected." But the perfection they sought was knowledge *(gnosis)* and not love. This heresy tended to foster a spirit of status seeking. A century earlier Paul had detected this danger in the church at Corinth, and John cautioned the readers of his First Epistle against it.

Another threat to New Testament holiness originated in Greek thought with its emphasis upon dualism: the antagonism between flesh and spirit. This led to *asceticism,* which believed that the greatest piety was achieved through rejection of the body. Asceticism was led by Anthony of Egypt, one of the pioneer hermits. It spread west until monasticism became, as Harnack described it, "the greatest organized quest for perfection in history."

Perhaps the most explicit witness to the baptism of the Spirit which cleanses from sin and fills with love, was Cyprian of North Africa. He testified to his own experience of deliverance and exhorted others to seek the fullness of the blessing of the gospel of Christ.

The most influential figure in the ancient church was Augustine, bishop of Hippo, in North Africa. His *Confessions* ranks as one of the world's best-known Christian classics of devotion. In it he expresses his love for God, recalling not only the grace of God in his own deliverance from sin, but the continuing presence of the Spirit in his life, leading him to explore ever more satisfactory relations with his Saviour.

John Cassian, a contemporary of Augustine, was an influential monk of Europe. His addresses to his fellow monks on the subject of holy living were among the factors that influenced Wesley's own development of the doctrine.

All during this ancient period the church was struggling to keep itself alive. It was engaged in constant struggle with those who would pervert the New Testament doctrine by false teaching from within, and those on the outside who would vanquish the church entirely by force. Nevertheless, this was a period of amazing growth and vigor. It is now regarded by Protestants and Catholics alike as the period of church history in which doctrine was formulated with greatest precision and care. Thus, both Catholics and Protestants affirm the creedal formulations of the first four ecumenical councils.[1]

The church during this period was also concerned with holy living. The anonymous Epistle to Diognetus defines the Christians by their unusual manner of life. The author pointed out that the source of their life is outside themselves, that their righteousness is quite unique and owes its origin to Christ. In short, he stated that Christians are to be distinguished from all others by their manner of life rather than by externals, such as politics, language, and the like.[2]

B. THE MIDDLE AGES (A.D. 500-1500)

For 1,000 years after Augustine, the light of the pure gospel shone dimly. It was confined largely to the monasteries and among the saints or mystics of this period. Among them may be mentioned Teresa and Catherine of Sienna, both of whom experienced the love of God to an amazing degree.

Francis of Assisi is another person almost synonymous with Christian piety. He is remembered as a Christian who thought it

1. Nicea (325), Constantinople (381), Ephesus (431), Chalcedon (431).
2. See K. Lake, ed., *Apostolic Fathers* (New York: J. P. Putnam, 1930), 2:338.

not sufficient to remain within the monastery; rather, one should be out in the world doing good as did Jesus.

From the 12th century came Peter Waldo, a merchant who was converted and became an effective evangelist, teaching the Word of God and preaching to the people. His followers, the Waldensians, still inhabit the southern portion of the Alps. Persecution by the church has not dimmed their witness. Individuals like Johannes Arndt, who wrote *True Christianity*, were lights for whom the Christian Church can ever be grateful. Arndt saw the difference between the decadent Christianity of his day and that of the New Testament. His writing influenced the Reformers, especially Luther.

The Brethren of the Common Life were similar to monks and yet differed in their monastic vows. Among them was Thomas a Kempis, whose book *The Imitation of Christ* remains one of the most influential books in the world. A contemporary of Thomas wrote the *Theologia Germania* (German Theology) which again bears witness to New Testament faith and which had a direct influence on Martin Luther.

C. The Reformation (a.d. 1500-1700)

While the mystics were primarily concerned with love to Christ and purity of living, others were also concerned with the truth. This dual concern for both righteousness and truth led them to become not so much mystics as reformers. Among them are John Wyclif of England and John Huss of Bohemia. Their love for God and for the truth led them to rebuke and expose error; this in turn made them an object of oppression. Only their deaths as martyrs terminated their continuing witness for truth and righteousness. Luther would have suffered the same fate as Huss had it not been for the German princes who had sufficient military and political power to challenge successfully the authority of the papacy.

The Reformation itself took two phases. One was led by the classical Reformers, Luther, Zwingli, and Calvin. The other wing included the Anabaptists, of whom Menno Simons is the best representative. The Anabaptists were the more radical and believed that discipleship meant that they should separate themselves not only from the organized church but also from the state. They regarded both the church and the state as dominated by Satan. Luther on the other hand looked to the state to protect him and his followers from the demands of the church. Calvin in Geneva brought the church and state together in a theocracy. This precedent was followed by the settlers of New England.

Later in the 17th century a movement which can be called the "reformation of the Reformation" was initiated by Spener in Germany. He was a Lutheran pastor who became convinced that purity of living was at least as important as purity of doctrine. As a result of his sermons, some of his congregation, who had previously been baptized and confirmed, were actually "born again." So he had a church of evangelicals within his state church. This was the beginning of a pietist movement that spread across the Atlantic into the New World and across the Channel into the British Isles.

The Quakers or Friends were a parallel movement led by George Fox. Fox was a "social mystic" in that he combined personal mysticism (direct communication with God apart from church and sacraments) with social concern and evangelism. He called attention to the essentials in Christianity and rebuked ostentation and hypocrisy. To his followers, response to the "Inner Light" (cf. John 1:9) was the most important element in Christian discipleship.

Meanwhile, toward the end of the 17th century the Church of England was experiencing renewal. The rapid rise of Societies for the Reformation of Manners doubtless reflected a reaction from the Restoration which saw Puritanism rejected and Charles II restored to the throne (A.D. 1662). These Societies within the established church were concerned with personal piety and a more vital Christianity than was prevalent. Thus, in England, Puritanism (outside the establishment and Calvinistic in theology), the Quakers (independent of both church and state), and Religious Societies (within the church) reflected a reaction from the religio-political wars of the 17th century. They followed the Reformation and prepared the way for the Evangelical Revival of the 18th century.

Jesus, plant and root in me
All the mind that was in Thee;

Settled peace I then shall find;
Jesus is the quiet mind.
Anger I no more shall feel,
Always even, always still;
Meekly on my God reclined;
Jesus is a gentle mind.
Lowly, loving, meek and pure,
I shall to the end endure;
Be no more to sin inclined;
Jesus is a constant mind.
I shall fully be restored
To the image of my Lord,
Witnessing to all mankind,
Jesus is a perfect mind.

—CHARLES WESLEY

Chapter 3

The Message of Holiness
in Centuries of Revolution

Some centuries witness much more change in Christian insight than others. The 6th and 4th centuries before Christ were centuries of great change. The same is true of the 1st, 7th, 16th, and 18th centuries of the Christian Era.

How has the evangelical (Wesleyan) witness reacted in situations of radical change? A common response in such crises is one of either accommodation or of resistance. An examination of these movements and reactions is in order.

A. THE 18TH CENTURY

The 16th century of religious revolt and reformation had passed into the acrimonious controversies of the 17th century. Forces of additional impact were on the horizon. The 18th century brought revolutionary changes.[1]

One year prior to the birth of John Wesley in 1703, the British East India Company was founded, an event which later led to the incorporation of India into the British Empire. The War of the Spanish Succession began in 1701; likewise, Queen Anne's War began in the American colonies. Also, Peter the Great was changing the face of Russia at this time. Queen Anne's War ended in 1713 with the Peace of Utrecht, resulting

---

1. "The eighteenth century witnessed one of the greatest political transformations in history . . . an attempt to destroy a social order, which men believed to be bad, and to create one which they believed to be good" (Walter E. Bauer, "The Philosophy of the American Revolution," in W. A. Quanbeck, ed., *God and Ceasar* [Minneapolis: Augsburg Publishing House, 1959], p. 117).

in concessions to England which laid the foundation for two centuries of British naval and colonial supremacy. England was at war with France during much of this century. Even the calendar was changed in 1752, the years thereafter beginning in January. During the second half of the century, England's victories on land and sea under the ministry of William Pitt continued. Clive of India led this great people into closer contact with Great Britain, culminating in the Treaty of Allahabad (1765) which established Britain's claim to India. Meanwhile, France lost all of Canada to Great Britain (1763). The war with Spain (1762) was followed soon after by the revolt of the American colonies (1775-83).

This century of change was climaxed by the French Revolution, a movement that seemed to threaten virtually every fixed value in the Western world. The goddess of reason was worshipped in the cathedral of Notre Dame, Paris, in 1793. The religious turmoil of the 17th century had been followed by the political upheavals of the 18th.

1. The Industrial Revolution

Equally significant was the industrial revolution that changed the face of Europe from an agricultural to an industrial economy and accelerated Europe's economic and cultural domination of virtually the entire globe. The rise of the capitalistic system brought greater prosperity but also a greater contrast between rich and poor. This coincided with the rise of a prosperous middle class, between the aristocracy on the one hand and the peasants on the other.[2] The invention of the steam engine led to the factory system during this century. Steam power also revolutionized transportation on both land and sea. The industrial revolution was now in full force, with the transition from handcraft to factory workers.

To this new and most difficult challenge, Wesley and his fellow workers were among the first to respond. It was George Whitefield, and later Wesley, who preached to the miners early in the morning before they descended into the mines. They did not wait for these people to come to the churches but went to the laborers where they worked. While the Church of England

2. J. H. Hayes, *A Political and Cultural History of Modern Europe,* (New York: The Macmillan Co., 1936), 1:93-95.

neglected these working classes, the early Methodists made the evangelization of the laboring man one of their prime concerns. Thus Wesley in his own words "made himself more vile" by preaching to coal miners, not in churches from which he was often excluded, but in the fields, as a part of his regular task.

2. The Intellectual Revolution

Along with the political and industrial revolution was an intellectual revolution. In Germany the movement called the Enlightenment was beginning to make itself felt. In France the Age of Reason was believed to have arrived. In England a constellation of intellectuals started off the century with a treatise by Collins on *Free Thinking* (1713). Wolfe produced a work on *Natural Religion.* Tyndale believed that *Christianity Is as Old as Creation,* setting forth an emphasis upon natural theology. By mid century David Hume, the great skeptic, was producing such articles as "Miracles," "Providence," and "Natural Religion" (1748-59). All of them were skeptical of supernatural religion. Higher criticism of the Old Testament began in the mid century with the publication (1753) by the Paris physician, Jean Astruc, of a source analysis of the Genesis account of creation.

Thus Methodism and the evangelical awakening occurred in a century of change, similar to the 20th. John Wesley reacted by referring to David Hume as "the most insolent despiser of truth and virtue that ever appeared in the world,"[3] and by writing *An Earnest Appeal to Men of Reason and Religion.*

3. Revolutionary Aspects of the Revival

As in any powerful religious awakening, there were certain revolutionary changes made in the religious situation in England by the evangelical revival.[4] There was a theological change which was very deep and extensive. Under the guidance of Wesley and other early Methodists, the quest for perfection turned into a joyous discovery which was followed, in turn, by a victorious witness and affirmation. There was a new emphasis

3. J. Wesley, *Letters,* J. Telford, ed. (London: Epworth Press, 1914, 1938), 5:458.
4. See Mildred Bangs Wynkoop, *John Wesley: Christian Revolutionary* (Kansas City: Beacon Hill Press of Kansas City, 1970).

upon the grace of God. With Luther, being on good terms with God was more important than being righteous.[5] Salvation was not so much freedom from sin as release from condemnation and the wrath of God. With Wesley, on the other hand, it was the love of God that was most fundamental. Wesley agreed with the Reformers on the depravity of man. But Wesley's emphasis was on grace as sufficient to bridge the gap between the holy God and a sinful man. Only as the Spirit possesses and enables one to fulfill the law is he truly saved: this was the emphasis of the German Pietists and of the early Methodists.

The Catholics through the Middle Ages had emphasized *infused* righteousness. It was obtained not by holy living but through observing the sacraments and by doing penance. The Protestant emphasis was upon *imputed* righteousness, through faith in Christ. By this they mean a righteousness attributed by God to the believer but not necessarily changing his conduct. The Wesleyan emphasis came to be upon *imparted* or actual righteousness by Christ through faith; this involved a change of nature. The Catholic emphasis on God's *love* exerted itself on Wesley through the Anglican church, in which he remained a member until death. The Protestant emphasis on *faith* was mediated chiefly through the Pietists, as well as through the first Reformers.

The Anabaptist influence, reflected in the Puritans and other independents, did not influence Wesley openly and overtly. There is little doubt, however, that it was a factor in his independent course with reference to the ordination of his ministers. An interesting question is whether the Anabaptist emphasis on discipleship may have influenced Wesley indirectly perhaps by way of his German friends and counsellors.

A radical thing about the Wesleyan doctrine of Christian perfection was that, unlike the Reformers, Wesley believed it to be possible in this life. Unlike the Catholics, he believed it was possible for everyone, not only for monks and nuns. Under this evangelical influence in Wesley's day religion became directly available to the masses, rather than being mediated to them through the church, or the hierarchy, or even the presbytery. Methodists were like the Quakers in this respect,

5. A. C. McGiffert, *Protestant Thought Before Kant* (New York: Charles Scribner and Sons, 1912), p. 24.

although they were more aggressively evangelistic. They were also more disciplined and under a better organization. Hence they were better equipped to respond to the changing social order.

There was also an *intellectual* resurgence resulting from the evangelical revival. This is seen in the multiplication of books and tracts which Wesley urged his preachers to use and distribute. Later in the century the rise of the Sunday school movement was again, in part, the result of this evangelical awakening. The Sunday schools, to a large extent, reflected an intellectual awakening, with a renewed interest in the Bible and in spiritual life. This interest extended to adults, so that the Sunday school in a large sense was an achievement in adult education. Both in individuals and in groups, a revival of vital salvation brings an intellectual stimulus.

Another revolutionary change, coinciding with the evangelical revival, was *sociological.* In the use of lay preachers and class leaders, Wesley was a pioneer in the laymen's movement. Laymen were not simply to serve the church but were part of the functioning organism itself. It was a movement that directly involved every individual and asked for his personal commitment. According to William Warren Sweet, the great revivals that swept England and the New World during this century, *reached the masses* for the first time in history. This was true in New England, in the Middle Atlantic colonies, and in the South Atlantic colonies during the mid-18th century, and on the frontier during the following century. This religious awakening gave impetus to reforms—sometimes initiating them, and at other times reinforcing them.

The spiritual movement of which Wesley was a part, often proceeded more rapidly than he himself was inclined to go. In many respects he was not the leader but the follower. He was a Tory at heart, a conservative with reference to social and theological changes. For this reason he viewed with great apprehension and displeasure the Revolution in the American colonies. This inherent conservatism accounts for his reluctance to leave the Church of England or to have his preachers do so. Wesley was nevertheless ever alert to detect the will of God by providences and by the leading of the Holy Spirit. He could therefore adapt himself gracefully. The gospel is always a revolutionary ferment in any unchristian social structure. Jesus recognized this and sought to give reassurance by saying that He did not come to destroy the law and the prophets but rather to fulfill them (Matt. 5:17). Nevertheless, the gospel preachers of the New Testament earned the reputation as those that "turned the world upside down" (Acts 17:6-7).

B. The 20th Century

The 20th century, like the 16th and 18th, is a time of revolutionary changes. For several decades prior to 1914 the world seemed stable and gradually improving. Revivalism, social reform movements, and missionary expansion characterized "the Great Century" (K. S. Latourette). Postmillennialism and the "social gospel" were then the prevailing moods. Liberalism in theology added to the sense of security and optimism with reference to man's progress. Then the world "cracked open at the seams." The brutality of World War I convulsed Europe and the world in a struggle for survival. Optimism reasserted itself when peace came in 1918 together with American Prohibition and the League of Nations. War was to be forever outlawed and temperance the prevailing pattern of civilization which considered itself Christian. However, this soon degenerated into the Jazz Age of the "Roaring 20s," the Great Depression of the 30s, and World War II of the 40s. The Slavic and Chinese peoples of Eurasia found themselves under the dominance of ruthless, atheistic Communism. For the first time in world history, some nations asserted officially, "There is no God." In a militant and dedicated Marxist ideology, Christianity faced its greatest rival since the rise of Islam 13 centuries earlier. Not only have these nations which defied God survived, they have grown stronger.

As startling as were these social, political, and theological changes, even more sweeping were the technological revolutions. The invention of the electronic tube probably ranks with the wheel as one of the two greatest inventions in human history. In the conquest of time and space, more progress has been made in the past 50 years than in the previous 5,000. By 1945, man conquered the world of *inner space* by gaining control of the atom and releasing the same energy that activates the sun. A decade later *outer space* had been explored, and some were calling for a "cosmic theology."

Paralleling this has been a social revolution. The rebellions that Edwin Markham predicted in "The Man with a Hoe" have now shaken the earth repeatedly: in the United States, in central Africa, and, to a lesser extent, throughout the world. No longer are the white or the western democracies assured of a dominant position in society.

Historians often cite the moral degeneracy of the early 18th century. But can anyone deny that much the same could be said of this century? Today many of the sins of yesterday are no longer considered sinful. This generation has gone far in the direction of those who did not like to retain God in their knowledge and hence cannot distinguish between right and wrong (Rom. 1:24-28).

What does the New Testament message, and its summons to holy living, have to catch the attention of men and to transform today's newly militant and arrogant paganism?

Already there are heartening signs. The adulation of such megalomaniacs as Mussolini, Hitler, Tojo, Stalin, and Nkrumah has been decisively effaced; these idols are smashed. The conscience of mankind is now more responsive to the evils of exploitation and oppression. There is a greater sensitivity to social evils and less of an inclination to tolerate them. Although the counterculture often continues to advocate violence to achieve its goals, there is a more widespread aversion to war and other forms of violence.

Certain leaders in Asia have been asking themselves how the message of Jesus, Paul, Luther, and the Wesleys can challenge and transform this generation. We do well to ask the same. The early Methodists were persistent enough to overcome adversaries and yet flexible enough to adapt to the changes of their age. We must do likewise unless we are content to let the Holiness Movement and the holiness churches become an irrelevant cultural lag.

What is the role of Christian witnesses in the world of change? The Hebrew prophets were spiritual barometers. They were attuned to the contemporary scene and also to the mind of the Infinite. They were interpreters of current events, exhorters, and foretellers of the future. Jesus and the apostles also constantly interacted between the changeless and the changing, between the temporal and the eternal. The early Methodists, with their dedication to the renewal of church and nation, were alert, flexible, resourceful, and courageous in confronting their countrymen with the gospel. We are in this succession. What can we do to "serve this present age"?

1. Holiness and Society

How do Wesleyan evangelical Christians stand with reference to the modern ecumenical movement? Shall we continue to be primarily concerned with building our own denominations, often at the expense of another, with little concern for the welfare of the total community? One holiness pastor excused himself from a county-wide crusade against liquor barons because he was too busy winning souls and building his congregation. Many of us are committed to pulling "brands from the burning," but we do not concern ourselves with "putting out the fire." Should we continue in competition or should we seek areas of cooperation and fellowship with other denominations? Will our witness be more effective in isolation or in dialogue? Can we or should we learn from those whose theology and practices are different from ours? Do charity and tolerance dull one's sensitivity to sin and error, and will they hinder clear discrimination and sharp distinctions?

2. Holiness in Human Relationships

To what extent is it true that the holiness movement in America has limited its influence almost entirely to middle-class Protestantism? To what extent are the large ethnic minorities, which comprise the U.S. "melting pot," represented in our schools, churches, and conventions? Does their absence testify to either our ineffectiveness or unconcern, or both?

It seems today that about the only issue that can elicit widespread moral indignation is the infringement of human rights. Why are not we adherents of "perfect love" and the golden rule more involved and more articulate with reference to racial injustice?[6] Have we, as Timothy Smith points out, been conformed to the spirit of this age, rather than challenging and changing it?[7] Have we permitted the liberals' preoccupation with the social gospel to dull our consciences in the presence

6. F. O. Parr, *Perfect Love and Racial Hatred* (Bourbonnais, Ill.: 1964).
7. Timothy Smith, *Revivalism and Social Reform* (Nashville: Abingdon Press, 1957), p. 211.

of deeply intrenched corporate evils? Are we geared to the issues of the present decade, or are we content simply to reiterate as "our distinctives" the truths that demanded utterance two centuries ago?

It sometimes seems as though our nation's leaders are more in harmony with the will of God than either the liberal or the evangelical churches. Liberals were the first to advise the federal government to urge admittance of Red China to the United Nations (and presumably to desert the then only Christian head of state in the Far East: Chiang Kaishek in Taiwan). The reason given for this counsel was expediency. *The Christian Century* advocated this policy for years. *Christianity and Crisis,* edited by Reinhold Neibuhr, urged the Allies to stop Hitler by force during the 30s. Later the same journal, headed by John Bennett, urged conciliation with the Communists in Viet Nam. Does this reflect ideological bias?

Have we evangelicals done much better? In the late 40s evangelical leaders urged rejection of the Declaration of Human Rights in the United Nations charter. In the mid-50s the same leadership warned against legislation that outlawed discrimination in industry on the basis of race. Still later, many evangelicals were hostile or indifferent to civil rights legislation. Similar groups opposed legislation designed to fix immigration quotas on the basis of individual merit rather than on national origins.

These things ought not so to be. Where should we take our stand on such matters? Does not the holiness movement have an opportunity and responsibility for showing the New Testament emphasis, avoiding both the humanism of the liberals and the reactionary attitudes of some fundamentalists?

3. Urban Renewal

Like most other groups, we have been building churches in suburbia, where we find "substantial people" who can support our church program. So far, so good, but who will minister to those remaining in the inner city? How interested are we holiness people in a spiritual urban renewal; with a spiritual transformation of "slums," whether in city or country? Should we be content to let renewal be carried on, if at all, only by the Salvation Army or by left-wing liberal groups?

And how inclusive is our concept of evangelism? Should it be limited mostly to Sunday evening services and special revival meetings? Heartening, indeed, is the trend among many groups to a multi-faceted evangelism—on the campus, in homes, in factories, and in the streets.

*   *   *

Ours is indeed a revolutionary age, but so were the 1st century, the 16th, and the 18th. The gospel of Christ is not necessarily hostile to change. Indeed, the gospel itself is revolutionary in its effect upon social conditions that violate the law of love. With good reason Jesus was suspected of jeopardizing Jewish institutions; His apostles were accused of "turning the world upside down." Christ not only tolerates changes, He often demands them. The liberal who welcomes change may be no further from Christ's theology than the conservative who is reluctant to accept Christ's teachings for change. The issue is not change itself, but whether the change is for the better—whether it is in accord with Christ's command that we love our neighbor as ourselves. In the historical context of our war with Mexico, a New England poet-prophet penned a trenchant rebuke to his countrymen. It is as relevant today.

> *New occasions teach new duties;*
>   *Time makes ancient good uncouth.*
> *They must upward still, and onward,*
>   *Who would keep abreast of truth.*
> *By the light of burning martyrs*
>   *Jesus' bleeding feet I track,*
> *Toiling up new Calvaries ever*
>   *With the Cross that turns not back.*
>
> *Once to every man and nation*
>   *Comes the moment to decide,*
> *In the strife of truth with falsehood,*
>   *For the good or evil side;*
> *Some great cause, God's new Messiah,*
>   *Offering each the bloom or blight,*
> *And the choice goes on forever*
>   *Twixt that darkness and the light.*

Though the cause of evil prosper,
 Yet the truth alone is strong;
Truth forever on the scaffold,
 Wrong forever on the throne.
Yet that scaffold sways the future,
 And behind the dim unknown,
Standeth God within the shadow
 Keeping watch above His own.

Then to side with truth is noble,
 When we share her wretched crust,
Ere her cause bring fame and profit,
 And 'tis prosperous to be just;
Then it is the brave man chooses,
 While the coward stands aside,
And the multitude make virtue
 Of the faith they had denied.

—JAMES RUSSELL LOWELL, 1844

The Christian can take revolutions in stride. He should, however, be concerned that they are not destructive of Christian faith and values such as the French Revolution and the recent revolutions under leadership of atheistic Communists. It is often said that the evangelical revival saved England from a revolution like that of the French. It would be more accurate to say that Wesley's influence helped to make the revolutions in England constructive, rather than destructive. Vital religion in the 20th century can and must do the same. The alternative is a resurgence of paganism and a retreat of Christian forces. But the Church is founded upon a rock, and the gates of hell shall not prevail against it, not even in the 20th century.

To serve the present age,
 My calling to fulfill;
Oh, may it all my powers engage
 To do my Master's will!

—CHARLES WESLEY

Chapter 4

Sources of Holiness Theology

A. Wesley's Spiritual Odyssey

Wesley's own theological and spiritual development is discernable in five stages.

1. Discipline—Holiness Desirable (1725-35)

In 1725, at the age of 22, John Wesley became convinced of the importance of holy living, and it became his lifelong concern. It was indeed his religious awakening, but Albert Outler is probably in error in calling this his conversion to Christ. He read much and learned from Thomas a Kempis (inward religion), from Jeremy Taylor (purity of intention), and from his contemporary William Law (complete consecration). At Oxford he joined the Holy Club and combined a quest for personal sanctity with social action. In 1733 he preached before the univerity his famous sermon on the "Circumcision of the Heart" dealing with Christian perfection—a sermon that he could endorse 45 years later.[1]

2. Disillusionment—Holiness Doubtful (1735-38)

He went as a missionary to Georgia, not so much to convert the Indians as to "save his own soul." But his strictness as parish priest met with resistance. His association with the

1. Sugden, *Standard Sermons,* 1:264.

United Brethren from Germany convinced him that he lacked assurance of his own salvation. He returned to England disappointed at having discovered even more poignantly than before his own spiritual lack and inadequacy for the task of ministry.

3. Discovery—Holiness Available (1738-40)

At Aldersgate in 1738 by faith he received for the first time personal assurance of his own relation to Christ. It was a heart-warming experience. This set the tone for all of his later ministry as theologian, counsellor, and evangelist. He now realized for the first time that salvation is a gift, not a reward.

Wesley also learned in Germany of the possibility of deliverance from inward sin, and preached that truth with great effectiveness to the multitudes. During this period he wrote *The Character of a Methodist* and preached a sermon on "Christian Perfection."

4. Definition—Holiness Experienced (1740-62)

In the theological treatises on *Sin in Believers* and *Plain Account of Christian Perfection,* Wesley defined his position. At a revival in London, in 1762, about 500 claimed to have received and experienced entire sanctification *after* they had experienced Christ in regeneration. Thereafter Wesley stressed, as a "second crisis," holiness available "instantly by faith."

5. Defense—Holiness Defended and Propagated (1762-91)

Simultaneously with the London revival (1762) the Maxfield-Bell fanaticism brought the doctrine of Christian perfection into much controversy. The Methodists were accused of "enthusiasm" (fanaticism), and Wesley found it necessary to defend himself against the charge of having changed his views when he urged perfection as a *second crisis.* To refute this charge, Wesley published in 1765 his *Plain Account of Christian Perfection.* It went through several editions, the last one dated 1789. In it Wesley provided evidence that holiness of heart and life had been his controlling purpose since 1725 when he devoured devotional classics and the Scriptures in quest of the "holiness, without which no man shall see the Lord." In the *Plain Account* he also set forth in considerable detail biblical evidence from Old and New Testaments in support of his position. It remains the most quoted source for Wesley's views on the subject.

The best concise exposition of Wesley's mature views on scriptural holiness were presented in 1765 in a sermon called "The Scripture Way of Salvation." A Methodist theologian described it as "a compact statement of Wesley's mature thought . . . of more practical value than all the other sermons put together."[2] In this sermon Wesley drew a clear distinction between justification and sanctification. Here is a recognition that sin remains in believers after justification, and here is the necessity of entire sanctification as available by faith now.

Wesley's emphasis on Christian perfection continued to the last. At age 82 he wrote to Freeborn Garretson, "The more explicitly and strongly you press all believers to aspire after full sanctification, as attainable now by simple faith, the more the whole work of God will prosper."[3] At age 87 he was equally emphatic on the subject of full sanctification. "This doctrine is the *grand depositum* which God has lodged with the people called Methodists; and, for the sake of propagating this chiefly, He appears to have raised them up."[4]

B. Divine Revelation

For Wesley God revealed His will in the Bible, in providence, in Christ, and in conference. The Bible formed a central place in Wesley's whole spiritual and theological spectrum. In his basic creed there were two main points: first, there is a God; and second, He has revealed himself in a book.

1. Scripture

Although Wesley was truly, as he said of himself, *homo unius libri* (a man of one book), yet at the same time he was an omnivorous reader. Habits of reading acquired in student days remained throughout his busy life. Unlike some of his preachers later, he was no man to disparage secular learning. One of his

2. *Ibid.*, 2:448.
3. L. Tyerman, *The Life and Times of John Wesley* (New York: Harper and Brothers, 1870), 3:462.
4. *Ibid.*, 3:625.

lay preachers burned his volumes of Shakespeare but not with Wesley's approval.

To the Lutherans the Word of God is that portion of the Bible in which God speaks redemptively. For them, therefore, there was a canon within the Canon; that is, a word of God enshrined within the Bible itself which is the Word of God *par excellence*. The Lutherans did not equate the Word of God with the Bible as such. To the modern fundamentalist the Word of God and the Bible are identical. The typical fundamentalist stresses the literalness of the Word and of each of the words. The important thing for him is the "Word of God written."

To the neoorthodox, much like Luther, the Word of God is that portion of the Bible which "speaks to man's condition." Thus, there is a subjective factor in the determination of divine revelation. For them not all the Bible is true, and even those portions that are true are not really the Word of God unless they evoke an awakening response in the reader. They point out, with some degree of plausibility, that the Word of God is not really authoritative unless one accepts it. Then they go on to draw the erroneous conclusion that the validity of the Word is dependent on man's response, reasoning from the false analogy that a sound must be heard before it can be a sound.

To Wesley, and neo-evangelicals generally, the Bible is uniquely authoritative and relevant. It is the unique and final revelation of God.

It has been stated that in the modern evangelical movement, those who insist upon an infallible Bible, or rather upon the infallibility of the original autographs, have been subverted by modern Calvinists. It is true that Wesley in his commentary on Matthew's genealogy acknowledges that the writer may have used erroneous sources, and that the Spirit of God would not necessarily have pointed out errors in the sources used.[5] As Wesley put it, "The evangelists . . . act only as historians . . . as they stood in those public and allowed records. Therefore, they were to take them as they found them. Nor was it needful that they should correct the mistakes, if there were any." Elsewhere, however, Wesley said, "If there is one mistake in the

5. J. Wesley, *Explanatory Notes upon the New Testament* (London: The Epworth Press, 1941), Matt. 1:1; 2:6; Heb. 2:7.

Bible there may as well be a thousand, and it could not have come from the God of truth."[6]

As McGiffert points out, "The debating of the authority and accuracy of the Bible was anathema to the early Methodists. Without hesitation they affirmed the full accuracy, authority, and relevance of the Scriptures." The emphasis today is not Calvinism versus Arminianism but the authority of Scripture, especially arguments for and against the inerrancy of the autographs.

2. Reason in Interpreting Scripture

The hermeneutical principles used by Wesley and his successors are important factors in evaluating their contribution to the contemporary scene. When Wesley wrote *An Earnest Appeal to Men of Reason and Religion,* it was his challenge to the sophisticated people of his generation. He pointed out in this treatise that there are two kinds of reason, natural and divine. Natural reason reveals nature, while spiritual illumination is essential to a knowledge of God (cf. 1 Cor. 2:1-16). Wesley stressed that the Spirit of God is the Medium of divine revelation. In other words, the "natural man does not receive the things of the Spirit." For this understanding, a man must have a special revelation; unaided reason is not enough. This emphasis upon the role of the Spirit was at variance with the spirit of his age, at least with those who said "Christianity is as old as Creation,"[7] and that natural religion is enough.

Yet Wesley scorned placing any premium upon ignorance. Instead, he urged study. He himself taught logic. He exemplifies close analytical reasoning in his sermons and essays. Wesley also scorned sophistry and all attempts at affectation. He sought the simplicity and directness of the First Epistle of John. As Hildebrand points out, "He would stand no Deism, no nonsense, and no 'dialectical' theology of the twentieth century type."[8]

Wesley scorned the 18th-century admiration for Jakob Böhme, whom Wesley's contemporaries placed "above the

6. J. Wesley, *Journal,* 6:117; 5:523.
7. Tyndale, author of a booklet by this title, published 1730.
8. F. Hildebrandt, *Christianity According to the Wesleys* (London: Epworth Press, 1956).

apostles." Of Böhme, Wesley wrote, "He quite spoils the taste for plain, simple religion, such as the Bible is, and gives false taste, which can relish nothing so well as high, obscure, unintelligible jargon."[9] If Wesley spoke thus about his contemporaries, what would he have said of the dialectical and process theologians of the 20th century? He would have abhorred the "death of God" theologians as much as he scorned David Hume, whom he considered "worse than a Turk or an infidel."

3. Experience

Wesley tested his interpretation of Scripture not only by reason but by experience. Both tests are useful. On one occasion he wrote that unless his doctrines were experienced by people, he would question their validity. On another occasion, however, he said that if this doctrine is scriptural, it does not matter whether anybody else has experienced it or not. The factor of experience played an important part throughout Wesley's life, and he remained open to evidence from that source.

In this he had a precedent in the New Testament. The apostles formulated their doctrine of Gentile inclusion on the basis of Peter's experience at the house of Cornelius, and the experience of Paul and Barnabas in preaching to the Gentiles (Acts 15).

With Wesley this dependence on Christian experience began when he was en route to Georgia. It continued when he was back in London, where at last at Aldersgate he had his own personal *assurance* of saving grace. After this he pursued the subject among the Brethren at Herrnhut, Germany.

Reference has already been made to the London revival in 1762. There some 500 witnesses professed having had a second definite work of grace resulting in the love of God filling their lives. Wesley closely examined and cross-examined these witnesses. He assured himself that they were not misguided fanatics but were sincerely and candidly reporting an accomplished fact. This experience was probably the most important single factor in his emphasis upon the *second* work of grace and the availability of perfect love instantaneously on

9. J. Wesley, *Works,* 1:514.

the basis of faith. In this respect Wesley was like a modern psychiatrist, critically testing, classifying, evaluating with scientific detachment. He gives one the impression that if these testimonies had not met the criteria of authenticity, he would have repudiated the whole matter.[10]

4. Conference

Another method used by Wesley in the exegesis of the Scriptures was Christian conference. He was convinced that there was value in conferring with other spiritually minded brethren. As the early Christians used the Jerusalem conference to settle a doctrinal matter, so the earliest gatherings of Methodist ministers were for the purpose of hammering out debated doctrinal points. *The Minutes of Several Conversations* reflect the theological concern and quest of these first dialogues. The conclusions reached then were the result not only of one individual's experience and interpretation, but were checked with those of his brethren. They studied, prayed, and talked until there was some consensus.

This is another respect in which the early Methodists followed the precedent of the early Christians and set a precedent for our contemporary appreciation of the importance of conferences. Then, as now, however, dialogue did not always result in harmony. Wesley's followers separated from the Calvinistic Methodists. In recent times persons in the Wesleyan tradition have found "theological consultations" beneficial in annual retreats. These have included the medical profession and teachers of social science as well as graduates in biblical and theological disciplines.

5. Tradition

Did Wesley believe that God revealed himself via tradition, that is, through the established church? Albert Outler stresses this with persuasiveness, but Wesley himself did not include

10. Cf. Stephen Neill, *Christian Holiness* (London: Lutterworth Press, 1960), p. 81: "Almost all 'Holiness movements,' 'Higher life movements,' and 'Perfectionist movements' of our time show plainly, if not always avowedly, their family kinship with that which began in the experience of John and Charles Wesley."

tradition in his threefold test of doctrinal truth.[11] This was an important matter in Wesley's day and has come to the fore recently in Protestant-Catholic dialogue.

Wesley was an Anglican clergyman; and Anglicans, like the Catholics, believed Christ revealed His will through the apostles and their successors in the church. Wesley accepted the Thirty-nine Articles of the Church of England. He minimized his differences with them while accentuating their validity.

In considering infant baptism, he tended to accept without question his church's position. The same is true of the sacraments. He acknowledged repeatedly his indebtedness to such luminaries as Aquinas, Taylor, Law, and others. He welcomed the help of the church and appreciated this tradition more than that of the Separatists and Dissenters, yet he did not appeal to the church to *define* evangelical doctrines. The Scriptures were the sole Authority for him. They were illuminated by the church fathers (especially the early fathers), by Spirit-guided reason, and by Christian experience. Tradition alone was never the determining factor.

Wesley, like all of us, was a creature of his age. He was also a religious genius who, influenced by the grace of Christ, was able to utilize his heritage, thus opening up new and creative spiritual forces. In so doing, he has left all of us in his debt for these two centuries and more.

C. Relevance Today

An important factor in any study of the Bible or of theology is one of contemporary relevance. It may be granted that perfect love is in the New Testament, but does it meet today's needs? Is it relevant? How does it stand with reference to the paramount issues of the day?

Dr. Ashley D. Leavitt, president of the Greater Boston Association of Ministers, while addressing a youth group, defined religion as "the life of God in the soul of man." This

---

11. Albert Outler adds "tradition" (Anglican church) as the fourth influence on Wesley's thought (Lectures at Asbury Theological Seminary, 1974). Although Wesley himself did not include "tradition" as a fourth factor, he often reflected it.

46

definition is an unconscious tribute to Wesley and to the early Methodist revival. Perhaps of no other religious movement in history would such a definition be more appropriate. The same thought is echoed in Charles Wesley's hymn,

> *Love divine, all loves excelling,*
> *Joy of heaven, to earth come down.*

That the vitality of the Wesleyan insights is still valid is witnessed by numerous doctrinal studies that are being pursued. It is also manifest in the vigor which accompanies those who are proclaiming this way of full salvation. Several missionary organizations in this tradition are expanding their field work at a time when others are retreating. Pentecostalism, a stepchild of the Evangelical Revival, is also continuing its impressive gains in worldwide influence.

The enduring influence of the thought of John and Charles Wesley on Christian theology was more important than they themselves realized. Neither of them were theologians in the proper sense of the term. They were concerned with theology and insisted upon its accuracy and importance, but they were not specialists in the formulation of doctrine. Nevertheless, their doctrinal emphases have been widely accepted, and they are taken for granted in many areas of the Christian Church today. Wesley was correctly termed a "theologian of experience" (George B. Cell) in the succession of Paul, Augustine, and Luther.

In Japan today, there is a renewed interest in both Wesleyan theology and the dynamic of early Methodism, witnessed, for example, in the emergence of the Wesley Translation Society. There is an increasing awareness among thoughtful religious leaders that Japan needs something comparable to the Wesleyan movement of the 18th century, especially in the direction of church renewal. A Japanese theologian (Noro) has called Wesley an "existential theologian." This is true in the sense that for Wesley, Christian experience was one criterion of sound doctrine.

Wesley was heir to the Catholic emphasis upon divine *love*, to the Reformation emphasis on *faith*, and to the Arminian emphasis upon free *grace*. He was sympathetic with the Anglican insistence upon the *means of grace*, and with the Pietists in their emphasis on *personal assurance*.

O for a heart to praise my God,
A heart from sin set free,
A heart that always feels Thy blood,
So freely shed for me!

Oh, for a lowly, contrite heart,
Believing, true, and clean,
Which neither life nor death can part
From Him that dwells within!

Thy nature, gracious Lord, impart;
Come quickly from above,
Write Thy new name upon my heart,
Thy new, best name of Love.

—Charles Wesley

Chapter 5

Distinctives in Wesley's Theology

A. EXISTENCE AND NATURE OF GOD

A recapitulation of the theology of John Wesley in the context of the 20th century has been done in Burtner and Chiles, *A Compend of Wesley's Theology*. William R. Cannon, in *The Theology of John Wesley*, places chief emphasis upon the Wesleyan doctrine of justification. The doctrine of sanctification in Wesley was dealt with definitively in Harold Lindstrom, *Wesley and Sanctification* (1946), and in Leo Cox, *John Wesley's Concept of Christian Perfection* (1964). Dr. Mildred Wynkoop has recently reviewed Wesleyanism as *The Theology of Love* (1972).

Because of his work as an evangelist and as an administrator, Wesley's contribution to theology is often understressed. It is true that he did not write a systematic theology nor a system of Christian institutes like John Calvin. So it cannot be said that his primary contribution was that of a theologian. He was content to make the theology of the mainstream of Christian thought, seek to vitalize it, and make it applicable to the masses. It was not his purpose to "do theology" or to "reformulate" it in contemporary fashion.

But Wesley's influence on theology was profound. He gave much of his attention to refuting the emphasis upon "limited atonement" in the Reformed theology of his day. It is significant that he entitled his publication *The Arminian Magazine* and defended its mission. In it he asked whether or not there were still some Calvinists left in the land who were opposed to the doctrine of holiness and who adhered to a belief in a limited atonement. Perhaps the most effective contribution in this area was his sermon entitled "Free Grace." In the sermon he labeled the Calvinistic doctrine of predestination a gross caricature of God and a disservice to the Christian faith.

The most distinctive emphasis in Wesley's theology, however, was his teaching on entire sanctification. Here he parted company with the mainstream of Christian theology and allied himself with the Pietist minority. Most elements in his theology are dominated by an emphasis upon the love of God expressing itself in the redemption of sinful man.

In addition to believing that God exists, Wesley was sure that God had revealed himself, and that this revelation is in a Book. He never ceased to be grateful that God in His sovereignty had chosen to make himself known to man. This emphasis upon God's self-disclosure is consistent with the Wesleyan doctrine of assurance or the "witness of the Spirit." It was in contrast to Catholicism and Reformation theology, both of which included a large amount of uncertainty regarding one's personal acceptance with God.

The areas of the divine self-disclosure are threefold. As the first chapter of Romans declares, God has revealed himself in nature. Wesley was among those alert to recognize in providence and in history God's revelation of himself both in judgment and in mercy. For Wesley, however, the chief Source of God's self-disclosure is in the *Bible,* which he accepted without hesitation as the infallible Guide and Rule, fully authoritative in every portion. He tended to equate the words of the Scripture with the thoughts of God. Wesely, however, was also a pioneer in his emphasis upon the witness of the Spirit, or self-disclosure to the individual. This came to Wesley himself upon the memorable Aldersgate experience when he received the inward witness that his own sins were forgiven and that he had a personal attestation of his acceptance "in the beloved." This doctrine of assurance came to be one of the most distinctive features of Wesleyan theology.

Another manner in which God reveals himself is in His providences, that is, in "his mighty acts" in old times, and in His daily "opening and closing of doors of opportunity," as with Paul and Silas before responding to the Macedonia call.

1. God as Creator

In his treatment of the attributes of God, Wesley produced nothing original. In fact, originality in theology would be furthest from his thought. What one needs to look for are the distinctive Wesleyan emphases and applications of traditional theology.

Wesley never doubted the existence of God. Even in moments of deepest depression, when his spiritual condition was at its lowest ebb, he still clung to two elements in his creed: (1) that there is a God, and (2) that He has revealed himself. Wesley would have had no sympathy for those self-styled apostles of the "death of God" movement. He would probably have dismissed it as a slogan which expressed in another manner what the Psalmist centuries before had declared: "The fool says in his heart, 'There is no God'" (RSV). Wesley's God-consciousness was in part the heritage of a devout home, where competent and godly parents gave him the best education which opportunity permitted. Wesley read, criticized, and commended Bishop Butler's *Analogy,* an apologetic which found Christianity similar to, but better than, natural theology. Divine revelation was necessary for both Butler and Wesley.

a. Among the attributes that Wesley mentions is the *eternity* of the Divine Being. This may be called one of God's natural attributes. Eternity is in the very nature of Deity. Even among the pagan Greeks, the gods were distinguished from men by the term *immortal.*

b. God's *omnipresence* was stressed also by Wesley. This is expressed eloquently by the author of the 139th psalm who says if he goes to the uttermost parts of the sea or even makes his bed in hell, he will find God there. Omnipresence was demonstrated dramatically to Jonah in his futile attempt to elude God's presence. Amos noticed that God's jurisdiction extends to the deepest Sheol (Amos 9:2). Solomon recognized that although he built a temple for God, yet the heaven of heavens could not contain Deity (2 Chron. 5:18). God is everywhere present, but Wesley noted that the language of the Bible accommodates itself to man's understanding. Thus God is often mentioned as being in a certain place. This problem has been brought into more acute prominence in the space age. Many decry the tendency to think of God as "up" there or "out" there. One is reminded of Paul's message to the Athenians, "in him we live, and move, and have our being" (Acts 17:28).

c. God's *omnipotence* is also noted by Wesley, meaning that He is all-powerful. The rabbis had a statement that "everything is in the power of Heaven except the fear of Heaven." They meant that God can do anything except force people to revere Him. It is difficult to reconcile God's omnipotence with His love, but Wesley seems to have devoted little time to this problem. It was a struggle faced by Habakkuk and Job, and it still seems irreconcilable to some people. A little child who can pray, "God is great, God is good," has a faith that many sophisticated people cannot claim.

d. God's *omniscience,* said Wesley, is "a clear and necessary consequence of His omnipresence." If He is everywhere present, it must follow that He is conversant with everything. It is characteristic of Wesley's presentation to content himself with biblical quotations supporting his point. There is seldom a philosophical discussion of these issues. Thus, Wesley can be said to be a biblical theologian as well as systematic. He could not be said to be a philosophical theologian.

e. The *holiness* of God was a favorite theme of Wesley. Holiness is both a moral and a natural attribute of God. Indeed, as presented in the Bible, it is basic to all the other attributes. Holiness is the very nature of God himself. Thus, holiness is not simply to be equated with goodness, but is rather to be equated with Deity. Because God is holy, He is without sin. It follows that He demands people to be like Him in this respect. It is the glory of Wesleyan theology to affirm with confidence that God is able to make men like himself. Like orthodox Christianity in general, the Wesleys believed that man, as originally created by God, was a holy being; and that in the Fall, he deliberately sacrificed this quality, preferring instead self-will. The falsely advised quest for knowledge led to a forfeiture of goodness. But the Wesleys also believed that "in him [Christ] the tribes of Adam boast more blessings than their father lost." In other words, full salvation can more than restore what was lost by man in the Fall and subsequent rebellions.

f. God is *just,* was a conviction of Wesley. This is often overlooked in his emphasis on the love of God, but Wesley was just as emphatic as any of his contemporaries in stressing the absolute justice and equity of the Supreme Being. Justice makes forgiveness difficult and necessitates vicarious atonement.

g. God is *love* is the crowning emphasis in Wesley's doctrine. His favorite book of the Bible was the First Epistle of John. This book more than any book of the Bible, fittingly typifies the Wesleyan emphasis. This is so because of its clarity, simplicity, and profundity. In this book, too, God's love is most emphatically stressed. Because God is love, said Wesley, all men may experience His love by faith in Christ.

In the Lutheran emphasis, God was pictured as Judge, and the most important thing in grace was freedom from condemnation. In Reformed theology God's sovereignty as Lord of the universe was stressed. This led, in turn, to an emphasis upon predestination at the cost of less stress on man's freedom and hence responsibility. The Socinians, and their spiritual successors among the Unitarians and other religious liberals, stress God's immanence, in contrast to the Reformation emphasis upon His transcendence.

The Wesleyan emphasis upon the love of God is in distinction from the Lutheran emphasis upon justice and Calvin's emphasis upon sovereignty. The stress upon divine love enabled Wesley to retain the balance between God's transcendence and His immanence, between His justice and His mercy. Love bridged the gap. In this, Wesley was in line with the theology of Paul (1 Corinthians 13), Peter (1 Pet. 4:8), and John (1 John 4:7-12).

Above all, God was recognized as a *Spirit,* without body or parts. This was common to the Articles of Religion of the Church of England and to the Westminster Catechism. It is in line with Jesus' emphasis that "God is a Spirit, and they that worship him must worship him in spirit and in truth" (John 4:24).

2. God as Redeemer

Wesley's main thrust as an evangelist was a stress upon the redemptive activity of God. He stressed both God's justice and His mercy in one sentence and in one breath. In a letter to William Law, he objected to the latter's statement that there is no judgment, anger, or punishment in God. Against the statement of Law, Wesley placed the word of God: "The just Lord is in the midst [of her]" (Zeph. 3:5); "justice and judgment are the habitation of thy throne" (Ps. 89:14); "I will punish the world for their evil" (Isa. 13:11).

But Wesley dealt mostly upon God's activity as *Redeemer*. He confronted his generation, especially the emerging working classes, with the announcement of the boundless love of God— God was willing to accept anyone who would seek Him. This message made a wide appeal to the masses because it was in contrast to the established church and also to the limited atonement of the Reformation theologians.

When Wesley's message was brought across the Atlantic to the men of the frontier, it sounded like a new gospel. The colonists were not accustomed to the idea that God loved all men and that all could find Him in saving grace.[1] The Presbyterians and Baptists preached a limited atonement and practiced a democratic church polity. The Methodists preached a democratic (inclusive) gospel and yet practiced an aristocratic form of government. Wesley did not minimize man's sin in order to stress God's grace. Neither did he minimize God's transcendence; but, rather, by his stress upon the grace of God he bridged the gap between man's sinfulness and God's holiness. This distinctive feature of Wesleyan theology has been missed in much of recent dialectical discussion.

To summarize, while many thoughtful persons of the 18th century thought of evil as only goodness misdirected, Wesley attributed the iniquities of the present world to a distortion due to the Fall. God made all things good but the Fall disturbed the good, and God's task as Redeemer is to restore the original condition of goodness through grace.

Wesley was convinced that nothing happens by chance, that even catastrophes are expressions of God's overall care for the ultimate welfare of His creatures. It takes a robust faith, however, to rest in this confidence. God's power and providence are limited only by limits inherent in creation and in the moral responsibility of man. God cannot contradict himself or force man to obey Him. His providential care extends to all races and

1. W. W. Sweet, *Religion in Colonial America* (New York: Charles Scribner's Sons, 1943), p. 318.

to nominal Christians as well as to genuine Christians. Wesley emphasized particular providences (answers to prayer) in a deistic age when this was widely doubted. While Calvin stressed the glory of God (in both salvation and retribution), Wesley stressed the righteousness of God in redemption.

Wesley's theology is essentially a biblical theology. He accepted some of the doctrines of his contemporaries but vigorously rejected others, on the basis of biblical teaching as he understood it. Wesley is relevant today precisely because the Bible is still relevant. Wesley, by providence, and especially by disciplined study and spiritual insight, was uniquely qualified to give wise and responsible definition to matters of theology.

B. The Son of God

Because of the Wesleyan emphasis upon perfection and love, the enemies of this doctrine have sometimes charged Wesleyans with neglect of the continuing mediatory work of Christ. This is not a true view of Wesley nor of Wesleyan theology. To the very last, both John and Charles Wesley would say, "I the chief of sinners am, but Jesus died for me." Wesley had no tolerance for any theology or system of religion that was not based upon the atoning work of Christ. He judged every theological pronouncement from that standpoint. Thus, Christology is central in Wesleyan theology.

However, the doctrine of the *person* of Christ did not receive major attention. Because of the Wesleyan emphasis upon the salvation of mankind, the *work* of Christ was stressed more than His person. This is true also of the New Testament. The Gospels say more about the work of Christ and less about His person. The same is true of the Epistles. It was not until the fourth and fifth centuries in Christian history that the person of Christ was the focus of attention. When, in the writings of the mystics or the deists, Wesley detected a lack of attention to the atonement, he would dismiss this as the equivalent of atheism or humanism. Not even William Law escaped Wesley's censure for an alleged neglect of the atoning work of Christ.

1. The Person of Christ

In his *Notes* on the Gospel of John, Wesley observes that "THE WORD" was taken by the evangelist from Psalm 33 rather than from Philo or any other heathen writer. The reason why Christ is called "the Word" by the Father is that He is the Only Son of the Father. He is, therefore, distinct from the Father. Wesley notes that the term "with" denotes "a perpetual tendency as it were of the Father and the Son to a unity of essence." The Son is styled God not in a relative sense but in an absolute sense. Wesley notes that "the Word" existed prior to all creation and, thus, without beginning.[2]

With reference to the *advent,* Wesley follows Paul in noting that God sent His Son into the world in the fullness of time or in the "middle of the world." When He became 30 years of age, the time priests began their public service, Jesus was manifest to Israel, speaking and acting in the wisdom and power of God. He not only knew no sin but did all things well, following not His will but the will of the One who sent Him.[3]

Wesley repeatedly emphasized that Jesus is Prophet, Priest, and King. As Prophet, He revealed the whole will of God. As Priest, He gave himself as a sacrifice for sin. As King, He has all power in heaven and in earth and will reign until He has subdued all things unto himself. As Priest, He is Mediator and Intercessor; as Prophet, He enlightens our minds and teaches us God's will; and as King, He reigns in our hearts. In his preaching, Wesley repeatedly presented Christ as our great High Priest who reconciles us to God by His blood and ever lives to make intercession for us. As the Prophet of the Lord, He guides us into all truth; and as our King forever, is giving laws to all those He has bought with His own blood and restores to the image of God. His reign in believing hearts continues until He subdues all things to himself; and, in the world of the cosmos, until He has brought in everlasting righteousness.[4]

In a letter written to a Roman Catholic, Wesley confirmed his conviction that Christ is the proper and natural Son of God, especially of "those who believe in Him, both by conquest,

2. Wesley, *Explanatory Notes,* John 1:1.
3. Wesley, "The End of Christ's Coming," *Sermons,* 2:72.
4. Wesley, "The Law Established Through Faith, II," *Sermons,* 1:6.

purchase, and voluntary obligation." He believed also that He was made man, joining human nature with the divine in one Person. He believed that after Jesus' suffering, in both body and soul unto death, his body was placed in the grave and his soul went to a place of separate spirits. He ascended to heaven, is seated on the throne of God in His mediatorial capacity, and at the end He will return to earth to judge every man according to his works.[5] In this Wesley followed, quite largely, the Apostles' Creed. In his emphasis upon the full deity of Christ, Wesley reports some unappreciative hearers, presumably the Unitarians of his day.[6]

In spite of opposition, he persisted in his view because he felt that the Godhead of Christ, the full equality of Son with the Father, is the foundation of all our hope. He explained himself further in his sermon "The Lord Our Righteousness" by saying that Christ is equal with the Father with reference to the Godhead, but inferior with reference to His manhood. He spoke of Christ's own righteousness as the "internal righteousness" which is the image of God stamped on every power and faculty of His soul. He described it as a copy of His divine righteousness, so far as it can be imparted to a human spirit. It is a transcript of the divine purity, the divine justice, mercy, and truth.

All this, he added, is in "the highest degree without any defect or mixture of unholiness." His "external righteousness" is both negative and positive. *Negatively,* Christ did nothing amiss and knew no outward sin of any kind. He never spoke one improper word or did one improper action. *Positively,* He did all things well; "In every word of His tongue, in every work of His hands, He did precisely the will of Him that sent Him." He "fulfilled all righteousness." In addition, His obedience led Him to suffering as well as doing. This is the *passive* righteousness of Christ in distinction from His *active* righteousness. Wesley added that active and passive righteousness were never separated; so that from either standpoint, He is called the Lord our Righteousness.[7]

The Wesleyan hymns offer another facet of his Christology.

5. Wesley, "To a Roman Catholic," *Letters*, 3:8-9.
6. Wesley, "Tuesday, April 5, 1768," *Journal*, 5:253-54.
7. Wesley, "The Lord Our Righteousness," *Sermons*, 1:1-4.

Most of the biblical terms attributed to Christ are found in these lyrics. Such epithets as the "Lamb of God," "the Lion of the tribe of Judah," "the Son of David," "the second Adam," are among the titles denoting the person of Christ. Thus Wesley sings:

> *Second Adam from above,*
> *Fill us with Thy perfect love.*

And again:

> *In him the tribes of Adam boast*
> *More blessings than their father lost.*

2. The Finished Work of Christ

In his sermon "Justification by Faith," Wesley dwells on the fifth chapter of Romans where Paul speaks of the second Adam as restoring the damage done by the first Adam. Christ is described by Wesley as the Head of mankind, a second-generation parent, and Representative of the whole race. As such, He bore our griefs, tasted death for every man, reconciled the world unto himself, and bestowed the free gift upon all men unto justification. This enables God to remit the punishment due to our sins and to reinstate us into His favor.

As Mediator, Christ stands between man and God to reconcile them and to transact the whole affair of our salvation. This, Wesley notes, excludes such man-made mediators as saints and angels "whom the Papists set up and idolatrously worship as such, just as the heathens of old set up many mediators to pacify their superior gods."[8]

It was Wesley's conviction that "nothing in the Christian system is of greater consequence than the doctrine of the Atonement."[9] This, he added, is the distinctive point between Deism and Christianity. Even though we cannot give a fully acceptable rationale of the atonement or adequately understand it, still we can accept it and believe in it. On this ground Wesley had to part company with rationalists who did not accept what they could not understand. Wesley insisted that to accept Christianity simply because of its moral teachings was

---

8. Wesley, *Explanatory Notes,* 1 Tim. 2:15.
9. Wesley, "To Mary Bishop," *Letters,* 6:297-99.

not real Christianity. God is angry with sin, yet He was reconciled to mankind by the death of His Son. Wesley added, "I know He was angry with me until I believed in the Son of His love." Also, "God was in Christ reconciling the world unto himself."

In some contexts Wesley spoke of man being reconciled to God, in others of God being reconciled to man. It is not clear whether he believed both were true or whether he failed to achieve consistency in the matter of who was the one reconciled. Paul spoke of God reconciling the world unto himself (2 Cor. 5:17-18). Wesley spoke of the sinner trembling before the tribunal of divine justice. Christ interposes; justice is satisfied. Sin is remitted and "pardon is supplied to the soul by the Holy Spirit who then begins the work of inward sanctification."[10] This implies that it is God who is reconciled.

3. The Continuing Work of Christ

The continuing work of Christ is that of Intercessor, Mediator, Priest, and King. Christ exercises rule in obedient hearts. As Prophet, He continues to speak God's message to the soul. In enumerating other continuing activities of the Son of God, Wesley says that He strikes at pride, causing the sinner to relinquish his self-will. In addition, He destroys the love of the world, saving believers from finding happiness in any creature. By destroying the works of the devil, He restores the guilty outcast to God, to love, to holiness, and consequently, to happiness. Finally, Christ will restore man to final salvation by the raising of his mortal body until it puts on immortality. By destroying death, He completes the destruction wrought by the devil. He restores man to the image of God, not only by deliverance from sin, but also, if he walks in the light, by filling him with the fullness of God. Wesley concludes that nothing short of this is the Christian religion.[11]

He notes further that the Son of God does not destroy bodily weakness, sickness, pain, and 1,000 infirmities. Nor does He destroy weakness of understanding which Wesley says is the result of dwelling in a corruptible body. These infirmities, he

10. Wesley, *Explanatory Notes*, Rom. 4:5.
11. Wesley, "The End of Christ's Coming," *Sermons*, 2:73.

said, have the effect of keeping us from a feeling of independency. However, even these will finally be destroyed at the resurrection.

He continues to add that Christians constantly need the mediatory work of Christ. Grace is received; it is a free gift as a result of Christ's purchase. This grace is not only from Christ but in Him. All blessings, Wesley adds, depend on His intercession for us, whereof we always have equal need. The best of men still need Christ in His priestly office to atone for their omissions, shortcomings, mistakes in judgment and practice, their defects of various kinds. All these, he says, are deviations from the perfect law and, consequently, need an atonement. Yet, they are not properly sins, since "he that loveth another hath fulfilled the law," for "love is the fulfilling of the law" (Rom. 13:8, 10). Wesley adds, "Now, mistakes and whatever infirmities necessarily flow from the corruptible state of the body and are in no way contrary to love, are not therefore, in the Scripture sense, sin."[12]

He emphasizes that the righteousness imputed to believers is not on the basis of any good thing that they have done, but solely for what Christ has done. Only by a free justification can we obtain or retain God's favor. He concludes, "My present and eternal peace are both derived from thee."[13]

*　　*　　*

Charles Wesley was more inclined than John to stress the element of prayer for added grace. John was more inclined to stress the climactic nature of two works of grace, while Charles stressed the continuing need for grace. But this is a matter of emphasis. Both of them equally stressed the moment-by-moment dependence upon the past and present work of Christ.

There is little that is controversial in the Wesleyan tradition about the person and work of Christ as such. There is, however, a continuing difference of emphasis about the work of Christ as it affects man. Is the righteousness of Christ

12. Wesley, *A Plain Account of Christian Perfection* (Kansas City: Beacon Hill Press of Kansas City, 1968), p. 54.
13. R. W. Burtner and R. E. Chiles, eds., *A Compend of Wesley's Theology* (Nashville: Abingdon Press, 1954), p. 87.

imputed or imparted to man? The answer divides along the line of Reformed and Arminian theology. This calls for a definition of Pietism, as contrasted to Reformed theology.

Pietism is a continuation of the Reformation, a "reformation of the Reformation." A younger contemporary of Luther, Casper Schwenkfeld, became convinced that Luther did not go far enough in an emphasis on victory over sin. He feared that Lutheranism taught a "sinning religion" by which the believer continued to practice sin even though he no longer incurred guilt thereby. Schwenkfeld protested an alleged tendency to antinomianism in Lutheranism.

Johannes Arndt published *Wahr Christentum (True Christianity),* which also called for holy living. The "father of Pietism" was Philip Jacob Spener, whose treatise *Pia Desidera (The Desired Piety)* called for a disciplined life of holiness. In it he stressed purity of life as even more important than purity of doctrine. (Similar protests against prevailing "dead orthodoxy" were later expressed by S. Kierkegaard and D. Bonhoeffer.) Wesley was directly influenced by the Pietists in Georgia, in London, and later at Herrnhut in Germany. From them he learned the importance of entire sanctification, of midweek devotional services, the class meeting, public testimony, and witness of the Spirit.

The Keswick Movement (in the Reformed tradition) suspects those in the Wesleyan Holiness Movement of minimizing the righteousness of Christ and overemphasizing their own righteousness. This criticism needs to be taken meekly and seriously. But the biblical (and Wesleyan) teaching is that Christ's righteousness makes a *real* as well as a *relative* change in the believer. Paul's emphasis on "Christ *in* you" means this. The message of the letter to the Hebrews is that the change is actual and inward, in contrast to the Old Testament experience (Heb. 9:14, 26; 10:10, 14). James likens it to the "engrafted word" (Jas. 1:21); Peter speaks of being "partakers of the divine nature" (2 Pet. 1:4); while in John, the divine seed *(sperma)* destroys sin because it is in God's children (1 John 3:8-10). This does not mean that it is a righteousness which is separate from the indwelling Christ. It is a derived righteousness and, at the same time, an actual sharing of Christ's nature (Gal. 2:20; Phil. 2:5; 2 Pet. 1:4).

C. THE DOCTRINE OF MAN

1. Freedom

Man has freedom and, hence, moral responsibility. For Augustine and Luther the effect of sin was in the bondage of the will. To them, man is "dead." Depravity is so total that man cannot even will to do the will of God. Augustine's contemporary, Pelagius—and Erasmus later—stated that unregenerate man is not "dead"; he is a "well" man and hence can perform good deeds. He has freedom of the will; there is no total depravity. While the Augustinians stressed grace at the risk of man's responsibility, Pelagius and Erasmus stressed man's responsibility with the risk of minimizing divine grace. To Arminius and Wesley, man is "sick." His is a limited freedom. The key word is *synergism*—man and God working together. Man's depravity is total in extent but not total in degree; not total to the extent that man cannot choose to do the will of God.

2. Sin

Wesley has been criticized by some contemporary scholars for having a "materialistic" view of sin. It has been said, by such scholars as Sugden, Flew, Sangster, Lee, and McConnell, that Wesley considered the elimination of sin as comparable to the extraction of a bad tooth. This they say in rejection of the concept of cleansing as "eradication." It is not a true picture of Wesley's doctrine of sin. He did not think of sin as materialistic, as anything inherent in the flesh. Rather, he thought of sin as an aspect of the spirit, centered in the will. His sermon on "Sin in Believers" makes this clear.

Wesley would not agree with Karl Barth that sin is "an ontological impossibility." Nor would he have committed himself to the Barthian notion of universal salvation. For Wesley, sin is rebellion—as it is in the Bible.[14] He accepted a moral dualism of the universe in which it was possible for a man to rebel against God and to remain rebellious. Thus Wesley was more biblical than Barth. Wesley would have agreed with some of Bultmann's emphases, namely, on the necessity for an

14. N. P. Snaith, *Distinctive Ideas of the Old Testament* (London: Epworth Press, 1944), pp. 74-81.

existential decision. What he demanded was commitment. As for himself, no sooner did he see the light than he followed through by acting upon it. Thus he was a theoretician but also an activist.

Most of the differences in the Wesleyan view of sanctification are derivative from the doctrine of sin, as Richard Taylor and others have stated effectively.[15] This is the chief difference between Wesleyans and other evangelicals. For the reformers, especially for Calvin, sin was any "want of conformity to the perfect will of God." This would include infirmities of the flesh and mind as well as defects of love. For Wesley, the emphasis was upon disobedience; sin was any defect of motive or of love, not a defect of knowledge or of strength.

Like those in the Reformed tradition, Wesley recognized that sin was twofold in its nature. For actual transgressions pardon was needed to remove guilt; for a sinful condition purity was needed to deal with the depraved source from which acts proceed. This, it was believed, would cure "the double-minded man" (Jas. 1:8) of his instability.

3. Assurance

In Wesley's day the doctrine of the Spirit witnessing to one's own standing with God, was regarded as fanatical. The bishop of London described Wesley's doctrine of assurance as "a very horrid thing." It was regarded as spiritual arrogance to claim God's favor or endorsement. Those who testified to being well-pleasing to God were suspected of being unbalanced fanatics. Wesley defended, both in word and in his writings, the practice of testifying to assurance. He encouraged the writing and publication of testimonies to full salvation. This witnessing was done on the street corners, in class meetings, and on the printed page. Among evangelicals today the doctrine is well accepted and no longer a subject of controversy.

15. Richard S. Taylor, *A Right Conception of Sin* (Kansas City: Beacon Hill Press, 1945).

Chapter 6

The Doctrine of the Holy Spirit

Next to the doctrine of the person and work of Christ, the most important teaching in the New Testament is that of the Holy Spirit. This doctrine is far more prominent in the New Testament than in either the Old Testament or in the intertestamental Hebrew literature.

From the standpoint of Christian theology, the doctrine of the Holy Spirit is the most neglected and yet one of the most important of Christian doctrines.[1] It is not easy to explain this neglect. Part of it is fear of fanaticism, part is due to an ignorance of human nature, and probably part is due to the fact that historically the doctrine of the Spirit has tended to divide Christians. The great division between eastern and western Christendom in A.D. 1054 was occasioned by failure to agree on the doctrine of the Spirit.

The person and work of Christ was the dominant theme of the 16th and 17th centuries—centuries of the Reformation. During the 18th, 19th, and 20th centuries, the major emphasis has been upon the work of the Holy Spirit. This is true with special reference to the Evangelical Revival of the 18th century and the awakenings of the 19th century. In the 20th century, Protestant leaders have also stressed the work of the Holy Spirit. Henry Van Deusen, in an article in *Life* magazine, described some of the younger Pentecostal-type churches as a "third major force" in Protestantism. It is significant that the

1. George S. Hendry, *The Holy Spirit in Christian Theology* (Philadelphia: Westminster Press, 1956), pp. 11-12.

fastest-growing branch of Protestantism is the Pentecostal movement in its varied forms. The Church of the Nazarene is also among the more rapidly growing Protestant groups; and it is probably more than a coincidence that among the Churches of the Nazarene, the work of the Spirit has been held always in prominence.

A. The Old Testament Teaching

A study of the Old Testament doctrine of the Spirit begins with a word study of the Hebrew term *ruach*. The word occurs over 200 times and therefore is a dominant topic of the Old Testament. In most instances, *ruach* may be translated "air" or "wind." It may also be translated as "spirit" and includes man's mind or emotions, as in Ps. 77:6, "I meditate and search my spirit," (RSV). It also occurs as "breath" in 39 instances. A good example of this is found in Ezekiel 37 when the prophet, viewing the "valley of dry bones," was commanded to say, "Come from the four winds, O breath, and breathe upon these slain, that they may live." As a result the dry bones received spirit and life. A beautiful thought is voiced in the opening chapters of Genesis when the Spirit of God brooded over the face of the deep, and "God . . . breathed into his nostrils the breath of life; and man became a living being" (RSV). The combined meaning of "wind," "breath," "inspiration," and "spirit" is illustrated also in Acts. At Pentecost we have the energy of the wind, the inspired utterance, and a spiritual regeneration. This combination of wind and spirit is seen again in the third chapter of John where Jesus likens the Spirit to the wind which can be experienced but not seen.

In the historical books (Judges through Kings) the prevailing doctrine of the Spirit is the *energy* from God which came upon selected individuals in time of national emergency. In this case, the Spirit's work was primarily that of energy in time of crisis (comparable to the injection of adrenalin into the bloodstream for physical energy). Judges such as Jephthah well illustrate this phenomenon. Note that the Spirit was not given for selfish reasons but only for community service. The gift also tended to be transitory rather than permanent.

In the "later prophets," or what we call the major prophetic books, the work of the Spirit is primarily that of reviving land and people as in Isa. 32:15; 44:3. Here the Spirit gives *life*.

The high-water mark of the Old Testament doctrine of the Spirit of God, however, comes in the prophets of the Exile. In Ezek. 36:25-27 is the great promise, "I will sprinkle clean water upon you, and you shall be clean from all your uncleannesses, and from all your idols I will cleanse you. . . . I will take take out of your flesh the heart of stone and give you a heart of flesh. And I will put my spirit within you, and cause you to walk in my statutes" (RSV). This prophecy probably lies behind the language in Jesus' discussion with Nicodemus concerning the new birth (John 3:3-9). Joel, in a similar vein, predicts the phenomenon which Peter later at Pentecost recognized as fulfillment of Joel's prediction (Joel 2:28-32 and Acts 2:16-21). The important thing to notice is that at Pentecost, as predicted by Joel and as envisioned by Ezekiel, the Spirit is given to all flesh, not merely to a few individuals; also He comes as an abiding possession and not a transient guest.

Although the term "Holy Spirit" occurs only three times in the Old Testament (Ps. 51:11; Isa. 63:10-11), the term "Spirit of God" occurs frequently. In the Old Testament teaching, the Spirit inspires *craftsmanship,* as with Bezalel (Exod. 31:3); gives military *courage* (Judg. 11:29); gives *authority* to kings, as when David was anointed (1 Sam. 16:13); inspires *prophecy* (Ezek. 2:2-3); and *cleanses* from sin both personal and national (Isa. 4:4; Ezek. 36:25). The purging of individuals by the Spirit is also envisioned in Ps. 51:2-10.

B. The Intertestament Period

The period between the Old and the New Testaments was relatively barren concerning the doctrine of the Holy Spirit, but any historical study of the doctrine needs to take this period into account. In books called the Apocrypha (Jewish writings included in the Septuagint but not in the Jewish Scriptures), there are only 10 instances in which the phrase "Holy Spirit" occurs. Even in these cases it is somewhat impersonal and not clearly distinguished from a purified human spirit. In the Wisdom of Solomon, for example, the Spirit of the Lord or the spirit of wisdom is said to "enter holy souls" (Wisd. of Sol. 7:22-27).

In Jewish writings other than the Apocrypha, many of which are apocalypses, the doctrine of the Spirit is neglected. This is especially seen in the visions attributed to Enoch. It is noteworthy that in apocalyptic literature the emphasis is upon God's transcendence. Angels, rather than the Spirit, however, are the normal media of communication or revelation. In the rabbinic teaching, which later was put into writing, the doctrine of the Spirit was expressed by a new term, "shekinah." The shekinah simply represented God's glory or God's presence. It was probably a carry-over from Ezekiel where the prophet in successive visions saw God's glory (the shekinah) move from the cherubim to the doorpost, and finally to Mount Olivet, east of the city (Ezek. 10:4, 19; 11:23). This movement typified the departure of God from the wicked city of Jerusalem.

The rabbis believed that the shekinah would not abide upon a soul that was sinful. In rabbinic literature the shekinah is comparable to the *real presence,* in the host at the altar in the Catholic churches. The evangelical Protestant equivalent, of course, would be the presence of the Holy Spirit in the temple of man's soul—"Your body is a temple of the Holy Spirit" (1 Cor. 6:19).

The Qumran literature presents an interesting doctrine of the Holy Spirit. Actually, this literature appears to be somewhat of a bridge between the Old and New Testaments in its emphasis upon the importance and the nature of the Spirit's work. There is, however, an emphasis upon the impersonality of the Spirit. One can never quite be sure whether the term "Holy Spirit" in the Dead Sea Scrolls refers to the Spirit of God or to the human spirit in which God is welcomed. However, in one remarkable passage in the *Manual of Discipline,* the cleansing work of the Holy Spirit is stressed. Here it states:

> God will purge all the acts of men in the crucible of His truth and refine for himself all the fabric of man, destroying every spirit of perversity from within his flesh and cleansing him by the Holy Spirit from all the effects of wickedness. Like waters of purification He will sprinkle upon him the Spirit of Truth, to cleanse him of all the abominations of falsehood and all of the pollution through the spirit of filth to the end that being made upright man may have the

understanding of transcendental knowledge and of the Lord of the sons of heaven and that being made blameless in their ways they may be endued with an inner vision.[2]

The inner cleansing then comes by the Holy Spirit, also described as the "Spirit of Truth." The "waters of purification" remind one of Christian baptism and of Ezekiel's prophecy, as well as that of Joel. In 20 places in the Qumran literature, the term "Holy Spirit" occurs. The need for the Spirit of God in the cleansing of the nature was emphasized as much as in the Old Testament and much more so than in either the Apocrypha or the rabbinic writings. Nowhere, except in the Book of Acts, is the cleansing from sin so explicitly linked with the Holy Spirit (cf. Acts 15:9).

C. The New Testament Teaching

1. General Review

From the standpoint of the doctrine of the Spirit, the New Testament reflects a mighty upsurge, an emphasis upon God being at work with His people. The word "spirit," which in all its varied meanings appears in the Hebrew Old Testament 203 times, occurs 386 times in the much shorter New Testament. The word "holy" is associated with "Spirit" 88 times in the New Testament as compared with 3 times in the Old. This prepares one to believe that Joel's prophecy was actually fulfilled in New Testament times and is reflected in the literature that the Christians considered uniquely inspired.

The work of the Spirit includes the *revealing of Christ*, as we learn from John 15:26 and 16:14—"He will take what is mine and declare it to you" (RSV). The work of the Spirit is also that of *revealing sin* to the unbeliever, as we learn in John 16:8— "He will convince the world of sin and of righteousness and of judgment" (RSV). The Spirit also *reveals truth* to the believer: "When the Spirit of truth comes, he will guide you into all the truth" (John 16:13, RSV).

Another major work of the Spirit in the New Testament is that of inspiring believers to *witness*, as we learn from Acts 1:8: "You shall receive power when the Holy Spirit has come

2. *Manual of Discipline* 3:13—4:26, as quoted in T. H. Gaster, *The Dead Sea Scriptures*, p. 53.

upon you; and you shall be my witnesses" (RSV; cf. Acts 4:31-33). Almost equally important is the work of inspiring the defense of those under persecution for their faith. Jesus told His followers to take no thought beforehand of what to say because the Spirit would teach them (Mark 13:11). In John's Gospel also, the Spirit is the Advocate (Paraclete) or defense counsel (John 15:26—16:15).

Finally, the work of the Spirit was that of purifying hearts of believers, as we learn in Acts 15:9 where Peter sums up both his experience at Pentecost and the experience of Cornelius by saying, "He . . . cleansed their hearts by faith" (RSV).

In summary, the New Testament presents the Holy Spirit as *illuminating,* giving *power* to witness, providing *courage* under persecution, and *cleansing* the heart from sin.

2. The Baptism with the Holy Spirit

a. Reformed Position. Because of misunderstanding over this issue, it seems well to devote considerable time to an exposition of the New Testament doctrine of the baptism of the Holy Spirit. The two major views are those held by the Reformed tradition and by the Arminian-Wesleyan tradition.

Among those holding the Reformed view are representatives of the so-called dispensationalists. This position is zealously set forth by John Walvoord and Merrill Unger of Dallas Theological Seminary, and by others also—including John Stott and F. D. Bruner of London and Manila respectively. According to this view, there is only one historic Pentecost and baptism of the Holy Spirit. This was given at a certain time in God's plan to the believers as a whole, and since this is an accomplished fact, the believer needs only to recognize it. Consequently, when a person believes on Christ and is saved, he is invariably baptized with the Holy Spirit. In the words of Unger, "The regenerating work of the Holy Spirit never occurs apart from his simultaneous baptizing, indwelling, and sealing . . . simultaneously, and eternally in the believer the moment he believes."[3]

---

3. M. F. Unger, "The Baptism with the Holy Spirit," *Bibliotheca Sacra* (Dallas Theological Seminary, April-Sept., 1944), pp. 232 ff. See also the extensive treatment in F. D. Bruner, *A Theology of the Holy Spirit* (Grand Rapids, Mich.: Wm. B. Eerdmans Publishing Co., 1970), pp. 155 ff.

In the Reformed position, the whole matter is to be interpreted in the light of 1 Cor. 12:13, "For by one Spirit we were all baptized into one body—Jews or Greeks, slaves or free—and all were made to drink of one Spirit" (RSV). This baptism is regarded as positional rather than personal and experiential. The emphasis is upon the objective rather than the subjective factor. In support of this position Mullens urges that there is only one such baptism—that described in Acts 2. The outpourings of the Spirit in the 8th, 10th, and 19th chapters of Acts, he argues, were "not baptisms of the Spirit" in the strict sense, but instances of "the reception by believers of the Spirit already bestowed at Pentecost."[4] In other words, the Pentecost was experienced in four historic installments: on Jews in Jerusalem, on Samaritans at Samaria, on Gentiles at Caesarea, and on disciples of John at Ephesus. It is to be regarded as one historic event and not to be repeated in the life of any individual believer since then.[5] These writers note that in the Epistles there is no command to be baptized with the Spirit, though there is the command to be "filled with the Spirit" (Eph. 5:18). In other words, every believer upon becoming a Christian is at that time baptized with the Holy Spirit; it is not something to be sought as such.[6]

A modification of this view sees a distinction between the sealing of the Spirit at conversion and the baptism or filling of the Spirit later. Some in the Reformed tradition are Calvinists who have been awakened by the Spirit and have walked in the light. Consequently they come close to believing in a "second crisis experience." Many of them say that this second crisis includes a filling of the Spirit, but it does not lead to entire cleansing from sin. The only difference between them and those in the Wesleyan tradition would be the issue of deliverance from all sin. C. R. Erdman states:

> It is undoubtedly true that there are those to whom the experience of being filled with the Spirit of Christ has come

4. E. Y. Mullins, "Baptism of the Holy Spirit," *International Standard Bible Encyclopaedia,* James Orr, ed. (Grand Rapids, Mich.: Wm. B. Eerdmans Publishing Co., 1939), 1:401.

5. J. R. W. Stott, *The Baptism and Fullness of the Holy Spirit* (Downer's Grove, Ill.: Inter-Varsity Press, 1971), p. 34.

6. J. D. R. Dunn, *Baptism of the Holy Spirit* (Naperville, Ill.: Allenson, 1970), *passim.*

to a sudden and epochal crisis. After long years of fruitlessness and failure some secret sin has been abandoned, some long neglected tasks undertaken, some definite surrender to Christ has been made, there has resulted a power and service never before experienced, a love for others never before known.[7]

In a similar manner, F. B. Meyer writes,

> Certainly the Holy Spirit has been at work within you, else you were none of Christ's. But there is an experience altogether beyond and above this initial step by which the Holy Spirit first reveals sin and Christ, and it is for lack of this that your testimony is now inoperative and your lives so destitute of fire.

Meyer goes on to note the difference between *having* the Holy Spirit and *being filled with* the Spirit:

> How many Christians complain of the uprising of their old depraved nature which so rapidly responds to suggestion of the tempter betraying the continued presence in the heart of that self-principle which is the cause of all the evil and misery of the world. This is largely because there has been no deep experience of the filling of the Holy Spirit.[8]

Thomas Waugh, in a book entitled *The Power of Pentecost* published by Moody Press, comes even closer to the Wesleyan position. He notes that the behavior of the disciples before and after Pentecost indicates "that the first effect of the baptism of the Spirit of fire is to destroy sin in the soul."[9] He adds that this does not come because of our efforts to cleanse ourselves but by making room for the incoming Holy Spirit. In a similar manner, Andrew Murray of the Dutch Reformed Church in South Africa notes that in every Christian church some remain babes. Others who are perfect or fully grown men "have their spiritual senses exercised in discerning good and evil."[10] These statements illustrate what happens when persons in the Reformed tradition respond to all the light in the New Testament.

---

7. C. R. Erdman, *The Spirit of Christ* (New York: R. Smith, 1929), p. 44.
8. F. B. Meyer, "The Filling of the Holy Spirit," in Thomas Waugh, ed., *The Power of Pentecost* (Chicago: Moody Press, n.d.), p. 116.
9. Waugh, *ibid.*, p. 59.
10. Andrew Murray, *The Holiest of All* (Old Tappan, N.J.: Fleming H. Revell Co., 1962), p. 62.

b. Wesleyan Position. One is surprised at the relative scarcity of materials dealing with the connection between entire sanctification, perfect love, and the baptism of the Holy Spirit in places where he would expect to find it stressed the most. In the Wesleyan tradition, it would seem that the *preachers* give far more attention to it than do *writers.* As Leo Cox and others point out, John Wesley himself did not explicitly equate the baptism of the Holy Spirit with entire sanctification, and subsequent to regeneration. However, what was implicit in Wesley, Cox adds, became explicit in such followers as John Fletcher and Adam Clarke—and later in Asa Mahan of the holiness movement in America, and in Pentecostalism.[11]

The advocate of the Arminian-Wesleyan interpretation of the New Testament would affirm, first, that the baptism of the Holy Spirit is distinct from water baptism, as seen in Matt. 3:11; Mark 1:8; Luke 3:16; John 1:33; and Acts 1:5. It is significant that Jesus baptized with water (John 3:22, 26; 4:1-2) as well as with the Holy Spirit. It would seem, therefore, that if the baptism of the Holy Spirit at Pentecost is only one isolated event in the past, surely the baptism of John should be also. However, if water baptism is to be perpetuated in the church, then the baptism of the Spirit should be perpetuated also. Nowhere does the New Testament teach that the baptism in the Holy Spirit as on the Day of Pentecost is to replace baptism in water.

If it be argued that the baptism of the Spirit is not a command that is emphasized in the Epistles, it may be added that neither is the command to be baptized in water prominent there. Contrary to Unger and Mullins, the baptism of the Holy Spirit in 1 Cor. 12:13 seems to refer to the initial water baptism and places stress upon the resulting unity. It is the Spirit who does the baptizing rather than Jesus baptizing in the Spirit. The stress there is not placed upon the baptism but upon the unity resulting from being incorporated into the spiritual body of Christ. This unity is in line with Eph. 4:4-5.[12]

In the Wesleyan view, the believers in Jesus were born of the Spirit (John 3:5; 13:10; 15:3; 17:8) but lived in anticipation

11. Leo George Cox, *John Wesley's Concept of Perfection* (Kansas City: Beacon Hill Press, 1964), pp. 122-25.
12. For other special meanings of "baptism," see Luke 12:54; 1 Cor. 10:2; 1 Pet. 3:21.

of His historic outpouring at Pentecost.[13] Caution is needed here lest a chronological sequence, caused by the gradual unfolding of God's purpose in fulfillment of prophecy, be too easily construed as the normal pattern for Christians today. Unquestionably, however, these men, now instructed to wait for the baptism of the Spirit, were already followers of Jesus. With Jesus' departure imminent, the need for the indwelling energy and wisdom of the Spirit became more urgent. Accordingly, both in John and in Luke-Acts, the disciples are prepared in a climactic manner both for the Master's leaving and for the Holy Spirit's coming.

In Luke 11:13 the disciples were taught to ask for the gift of the Spirit. In Luke 24:49 Jesus promised that He would soon send "the promise of my Father" which would clothe them with "power from on high." In Acts 1:4 they were exhorted to "wait for the promise of the Father." That this promised Gift is identical with the baptism of the Holy Spirit is evident from Acts 1:5, "But before many days you shall be baptized with the Holy Spirit" (RSV). Its fulfillment is recorded in the words of Peter, "Having received from the Father the promise of the Holy Spirit, he has poured out this" (Acts 2:33, RSV). It is important to note that this "promise of the Father" was given to disciples, not to unbelievers. The gift was to make effective the witness of those who were already children of the Kingdom (Luke 10:20).[14] Pentecost is not presented as initiation into discipleship; rather it brings purifying (Acts 15:9) and empowering (Acts 1:8) to those already discipled or converted.

It is the work of the Spirit to awaken and enlighten the unsaved as to his sinful condition and need of salvation (John 16:8-11; Rom. 8:9; Gal. 3:2). The Spirit also comes to every believer at conversion, creating within him a new heart, revealing Christ as Saviour, sealing him unto the day of redemption, and witnessing to his adoption into the family of God.[15] Henceforth, as he walks "in the light," he is a participant in the "Spirit-bearing community," the *koinonia* (1 John 1:3; cf. 2:20).

13. For fuller treatment of "The Wesleyan View" see C. W. Carter, *The Person and Ministry of the Holy Spirit* (Grand Rapids, Mich.: Baker Book House, 1974), pp. 178-89.

14. Contrary to Dunn, of *ibid.*, pp. 90 ff.

15. "Any one who does not have the Spirit of Christ does not belong to him" (Rom. 8:9; cf. 8:16; 2 Cor. 5:17; Eph. 1:13; 4:30).

But subsequent to this the believer needs to be "sanctified through the truth," "filled with the Spirit," and "endued with power from on high" (John 17:17; Eph. 5:18; Luke 24:49). The 11 disciples had received the Holy Spirit when Jesus "breathed upon them" after the Resurrection (John 20:22), but they still needed the infilling, cleansing, and empowering of the Spirit. Peter, in reviewing the outpouring of the Spirit at Pentecost, and subsequently at the home of Cornelius, summed it up as having "cleansed their hearts by faith" (Acts 15:9, RSV). This was more than inclusion into the Christian community—more than a rite of initiation; it was an enduement of "power from on high" for the purpose of witnessing (Luke 24:49; Acts 1:4-8).

The work of the Spirit also effects the believer's regeneration (John 3:5; Titus 3:5). Sanctification thus begins at conversion and is carried on actively in the soul as long as that person is in touch with Christ. This is what is meant by Titus 3:5, "the washing of regeneration and renewal in the Holy Spirit" (RSV). The word "renew" occurs four times in the New Testament and the passages are concerned primarily with the regenerating work of the Holy Spirit which otherwise is called progressive sanctification (Rom. 12:1; 2 Cor. 4:16; Col. 3:10; Titus 3:5).

The work of the Spirit in *entire* sanctification is seen in Acts 15:9 where Peter summed up the significance of Pentecost and also his experience in Cornelius' home by saying, "He [God] made no distinction between us and them, but cleansed their hearts by faith" (RSV). This is perhaps the only text in the New Testament that directly and explicitly links cleansing with the work of the Holy Spirit. However, cleansing is implied elsewhere as has often been noted.

The results of Pentecost in the disciples "before and after" strongly implies the work of entire sanctification. In spite of the fact that their names were written in heaven and hence we would call them *converted* prior to Pentecost, still they had many evidences of "the old nature." They showed worldly attitudes such as intolerance, pride, selfishness, race prejudices, and fear. To all of these they present marked contrasts after Pentecost.

What contribution did Wesley make to the doctrine of the Holy Spirit? In Lutheran theology the Spirit was given through the sacraments, much the same as in Catholicism; hence, the importance of the Eucharist as the "Real Presence." In Calvin the emphasis was upon the witness of the Spirit in the written Word. For this reason the Reformed tradition places great emphasis upon the words in the Bible; it is there that the Spirit bears His witness.

With the Quakers, the emphasis was upon the direct witness of the Spirit, with correspondingly less emphasis upon the written Word. This is seen in George Fox's emphasis upon the "Inner Light," and is reflected in Barclay's *Theses.* Wesley held a mediating position between the Calvinists and the Quakers. He stressed the witness of the Spirit, but that witness was subordinate to the written Word.

For Wesley the witness of the Spirit was not so much a witness to the veracity of the written Word, as with Calvin. Rather it was to the reality of the individual's state of grace, as with Paul and John, "The Spirit . . . beareth witness with our spirit, that we are the children of God" (Rom. 8:16; cf. 1 John 3:19-21; 4:2-6, 13).

Greater stress could well have been placed by Wesley upon the power of the Spirit for effective service and upon the purifying work of the Spirit in entire sanctification. Nevertheless, it is in this Wesleyan tradition that today's greatest emphasis lies upon these works of the Spirit, especially as emphasized in the Acts of the Apostles.

Those in this tradition have shown relatively little concern with spiritual gifts, reflecting Paul's position in 1 Corinthians 12 and 14.[16] In this respect most modern Wesleyans seem to follow the Pauline emphasis, in which the gifts of the Spirit are considered less important than the graces of the Spirit (Gal. 5:22-25). Schleiermacher correctly observed that the fruits of the Spirit are the virtues of Christ. The gifts are given; grace is to be sought.

D. SUMMARY

It would be correct to say that in Johannine writings the work of the Spirit as *Teacher* is stressed. In the Synoptics and

16. Recently there has been an overdue recognition that all those "in Christ" are given gifts of the Spirit for effective service (Rom. 12:3-8; 1 Cor. 12:12-31; Eph. 4:4-16).

Acts, the *power* of the Spirit is prominent, while Paul's Epistles emphasized the *purifying* of the Spirit. The Corinthians were concerned with the charismatic aspect of the Spirit's work in His numerous gifts. The apostle was even more concerned with the ethical effects of holy living when he said, "If we live by the Spirit, let us also walk by the Spirit" (Gal. 5:25, RSV). Paul would say that the spiritual man is judged not by his abundance of gifts but by his righteous life-style (1 Corinthians 13). Perhaps the holiness movement can concern itself with no more important problem than keeping these three emphases in perspective—the work of the Spirit in *illuminating, empowering,* and *purifying.* One is certainly in line with Paul's great concern when he remembers that the graces of the Spirit are more important than the gifts of the Spirit, and that the most spiritual person is the one who is most Christlike. Let us therefore rejoice that the "Comforter has come."

O spread the tidings 'round, wherever man is found,
Wherever human hearts and human woes abound;
Let every Christian tongue proclaim the joyful sound:
  The Comforter has come!

O boundless love divine! how shall this tongue of mine
To wond'ring mortals tell the matchless love divine—
That I, a child of hell, should in His image shine!
  The Comforter has come!

The Comforter has come, The Comforter has come!
The Holy Ghost from heav'n, The Father's promise giv'n.
O spread the tidings 'round, Wherever man is found—
  The Comforter has come!

—F. BOTTOME

Certainly the church, and hence the world, has no need greater than that of being entirely sanctified and filled with the Holy Spirit. Such was the case in the first century as evidenced in the Acts of the Apostles. We need to be Spirit-filled today to have an effective witness to the world. We need also to be Spirit-filled to have a witness to those church groups which have largely lost their message and mission. As one church leader acknowledged, after comparing the progress of the newer groups

76

with the stagnation of the older denominations, "I guess we need more 'spizerinctum.'" A Spirit-filled church would be the answer to his dilemma.

How can we be filled with the Spirit? First, by *confession* of spiritual need: "Blessed are the poor in spirit." A confession by the child of God that he needs the filling and cleansing power of the Spirit is as essential as for the sinner to confess his sin. Second, *petition* is important: "How much more shall your heavenly Father give the Holy Spirit to them that ask him?" Third, *consecration:* "To the extent that we consecrate, the Spirit sanctifies." The sinner surrenders; but the child of God can dedicate his will, his all, himself. Fourth is *trust:* Faith is the avenue of every blessing. Trust the Lord to accept the vessel now offered to Him, to cleanse and to fill it for His exclusive use!

> *O come and dwell in me,*
> *Spirit of pow'r within!*
> *And bring the glorious liberty*
> *From sorrow, fear, and sin.*
>
> *Hasten the joyful day*
> *Which shall my sins consume,*
> *When old things shall be done away,*
> *And all things new become.*
>
> *I ask no higher state;*
> *Indulge me but in this,*
> *And soon or later then translate*
> *To my eternal bliss.*
>
> —CHARLES WESLEY

Chapter 7

Christian Holiness
and Individual Experience

There are practical matters in the realm of the theory and experience of Christian perfection that keep recurring in individual experience. They are often brought out in conference with inquiries. Sometimes the need is expressed most insistently where it would least be expected and among those who are supposed to be best informed and most mature.

An honest seeker sometimes asks: "Actually what practical difference does the doctrine and experience of perfect love make? Are there not devout and effective Christian workers who do not stress holiness as a second definite work of grace? Are not their lives sometimes superior to those of adherents to the Wesleyan position?"

Another will ask, "What is the difference between holy and unholy anger, or is all anger sinful?" Again, one may wonder how to distinguish between sinful inclinations and human weakness. How can one distinguish between a tendency to evil and a temptation?

Still another wonders how one can be entirely sanctified and yet lose this experience almost unconsciously. If holiness of heart can be obtained only by conscious seeking, how can it be lost unconsciously and unintentionally?

Still others ask, "Is *eradication* a good term to describe

what God does in entire sanctification, or are the terms *suppression* or *inhabitation* preferable?" Clarification at points such as these is needed.

A. What God Does Not Expect

We do well to inquire what Christian perfection is not. The older apologists for this doctrine would say that it is not the perfection of angels, nor of God, nor absolute perfection, but a relative perfection appropriate for man in his present condition. Today we may add that it is not noise or excitement, though both noise and excitement often accompany extraordinary visitations of divine grace. A woman in Appalachia was heard to say concerning an evangelist, "I don't care what he says as long as he says it loud." Many fail to distinguish between *spiritual* and *spirited.*

It may also be affirmed that Christian maturity is not measured by speaking in an unknown tongue. It is true that the gift of tongues is one of the spiritual gifts mentioned in the New Testament. But much modern glossolalia, unlike the kind that Paul commended, seldom edifies and enlightens. Rather it often serves to inflate the possessor and to alienate the onlooker. It does not fulfill the Pauline qualification of edification. That which is unintelligible can hardly be said to edify (1 Cor. 14:4-12).

Nor is perfect love measured simply in terms of plainness alone; or of ugliness. Holiness is not to be equated with rudeness. Although many of the ancient ascetics regarded cleanliness as worldliness, there is no justification for this link. Perfect love does not unnecessarily offend. Eccentricity is not a hallmark of one possessing sanctifying grace. The ability to handle poisonous serpents without being harmed is not an evidence of an advanced state of Christian saintliness. The one scripture text cited in support of this practice (Mark 16:18) is probably not a part of the original Gospel by Mark; and even if we accept the account as an inspired record, it was not done as a stunt for exhibitionism.

Extreme asceticism is not necessarily a mark of superior devotion. Ascetic practices result from the introduction into Christianity of an alien dualism that is not part of the Christian gospel. Nor is abject servility necessarily evidence of humility or of piety. These are *not* criteria of perfect love.

B. What Christian Perfection Includes

Poverty of spirit. A person who has been made perfect in love is one who is delivered from a feeling of sinful self-sufficiency. He is not only poor in spirit, but he recognizes it. He has no righteousness of his own to claim or to trust in. Such a person is apt to pray,

> *I ask no dream, no prophet ecstasies,*
> *No sudden rending of the veil of clay,*
> *No angel visitant, no opening skies;*
> *But take the dimness of my soul away.*
> —George Croly (1780-1860)

Meekness. Christian perfection involves meekness (Matt. 5:5). This quality in perfect love is not vindictive nor self-assertive. It is content to commit, to trust, and sometimes to wait. David exhibited this spirit when beset by Saul; though promised the kingdom, he refrained from taking advantage of his enemy and waited God's good time.

Humility. Linked with meekness is humility. It is the opposite of being "puffed up," as were the Corinthians (1 Cor. 5:2; 8:1; 13:5). It does not seek ostentation in dress, in homes, in automobiles, in honorary degrees, or otherwise. It appreciates recognition, but does not demand it, nor become resentful when it is not forthcoming.

Simplicity. Another important ingredient is simplicity (Matt. 6:2-6). It does not make long prayers for publicity purposes when a shorter one will suffice. It does not use polysyllabic words if a simple vocabulary will serve as well or better. It does not seek recognition or commendation for generosity. Its security is in God and not in wealth. It does not place its trust in material possessions, but rather does "lay up . . . treasures in heaven." It is quick to recognize the hazards of materialism, quick to mark the appearance of covetousness, and quick to repudiate it. It has a quality of non-affectation, of candor—a willingness to be known for what one is rather than insisting on being overrated. It places pleasing God on a higher plane than pleasing men. It is free from the pride of face, of race, of place, and of grace. It does not bid for the limelight, nor become restive when unnoticed, nor resentful even when unappreciated.

Purity. Perfect love is characterized by purity of heart (Matt. 5:8). Jesus said that if one's eye is single, his whole body shall be full of light; and James declares, "The double-minded man is unstable in all his ways." "Purity of heart," said Kierkegaard, "is to will one thing." The pure in heart, and only they, shall see the Lord. This purity means freedom from indwelling sin, freedom from anything that is contrary to Christ's teaching or contrary to His love. It is natural for God's children to desire purity, to seek it and to praise it, to give it highest priority.

As purity is one of the main ingredients in a happy marriage, so we are told in the Scriptures that Christ, when taking the Church as His Bride, "cleansed her by the washing of water with the word, that he might present the church to himself in splendor, without spot or wrinkle or any such thing, that she might be holy and without blemish" (Eph. 5:26-27, RSV).

Courage. On the more positive side, Christian perfection has an important ingredient of courage. This is often played down by exponents of full salvation, but it is a virtue easily overlooked. Jesus manifested it on more than one occasion, especially when arrested in the Garden of Gethsemane. Peter and John demonstrated it when called before the same council that was responsible for Jesus' death. These two apostles, at the risk of life, reaffirmed their decision to preach the gospel. In addition to courage under adversity, God's ideal Christian is one who, because he is filled with the Spirit, is equipped with power for witnessing (Acts 1:8). He then becomes simply a channel, and the power working in him is not of himself but of God. When dedicated to God and filled with the Spirit, man's native capacity is multiplied manyfold. He finds an effectiveness that would otherwise be foreign to him.

Patience. The person who fulfills the qualification of God's man is a man of patience. Often this spirit is the result of trial, as well as coming from the removal of evil. And there is a time factor in patience. James urges that temptations be accepted in stride so that patience may "have its full effect, that you may be perfect and complete, lacking in nothing" (Jas. 1:4, RSV). Paul prayed that the Colossians might have "endurance and patience with joy" (Col. 1:11, RSV).

Power. Christians are to be fruitful and effective. The Gospels, the Acts, and the Epistles link power with life in the Spirit. Five Greek synonyms for "power" appear in Eph. 1:15-22. The "promise of the Father" (Acts 1:4, 8) resulted in effective witnessing "with great power" (Acts 4:33). From the same source comes power to resist evil (Eph. 6:10-11; Col. 1:11).

In addition, there is cohesive *divine love* which binds all together, and which provides the capsheaf to the other virtues (Col. 3:14; 1 Pet. 4:8). This is the one indispensable virtue, even outranking faith and hope—though it never exists without them. Paul insists that love far outclasses such things as prophecy, knowledge, and tongues (1 Corinthians 12—14).

C. Criticisms of the Movement from Without

The accusation is sometimes voiced that advocates of "second blessing holiness" in practice teach "once in grace always in grace." After they have received their second blessing, if in some area they fall short of the ideal, they go on professing anyway. They try to persuade themselves that a fit of anger is nervousness rather than carnality, or they justify the display of pride as simply a human trait. This is sometimes a just criticism. It should not be rejected or ignored, but prayerfully faced. Should we not "watch and pray, lest [we] . . . enter into temptation"? And if we should sin, let us remember that "we have an advocate with the Father, Jesus Christ the righteous," and avail ourselves immediately of His grace.

Another accusation is that those who profess entire sanctification place themselves in a category superior to other Christians. Thus they are said to aggrandize themselves and disparage others who cannot claim this experience. This argument has no more validity than for one to say that we should not profess to be born again because there are some in the church who cannot make this claim. It is true that one should not regard himself as superior, but should he not be explicit and clear in his relationship to Christ, and should he hesitate to declare with gratitude what Christ has done for his soul?

Perfection is said to be an unscriptural and practically impossible ideal. In almost any audience a preacher can be expected to have support if he disclaims any sympathy with what he calls "perfectionism." In answer it may be said that this is a rather loose way of describing adherents of the Wesleyan position, because the current English term *perfect* means "flawless." Christian perfection needs to be defined constantly and clearly, in biblical concepts, as a relative and not an absolute perfection. It would be well not to use this term to the exclusion of others, but to use also such terms as *blamelessness, wholeheartedness, purity of heart,* and *perfection of love.* Furthermore, the term *perfection* should always be qualified by the adjectives *Christian, evangelical,* or *biblical.*

Critics of the doctrine say that is advocates base their theories upon a very weak exegesis. They tend to substitute their own experience or the experiences of associates for solid scriptural exegesis. This may be a valid criticism. Holiness preachers are well advised to spend more time on exegesis and to rely less on anecdotes, analogies, and polemics. There is no substitute for solid exegesis of the Bible and for expository preaching. This calls for more than the quoting of a few proof texts.

It has been said that this experience fosters pride. Niebuhr referred contemptuously to "pretentions to perfection." This may be true of some, but it need not be true of any. Certainly this was not true of Wesley nor of most of his followers; neither is it true today as a generalization. Christian perfection, or perfect love shed abroad in the heart, instead of making one proud, causes one to "pour contempt on all . . . [his] pride" as he beholds the Cross.

It has been noticed by some that the profession of full salvation tends to discourage candor in its professors. They are reluctant to say that they have fallen short or have sinned; to do so would jeopardize their profession. This is often all too true. However, the remedy is simply honesty, earnestness, and walking in the light by faith.

Few of these criticisms are new; they have been faced for two centuries. Also criticisms are heard less frequently now, perhaps because there are fewer witnesses to this experience, or perhaps because the teaching has become better accepted and tends to be taken for granted. It is no longer new and excites less curiosity and hostility. Also its present-day adherents probably are less critical of other viewpoints and in turn incur less overt hostility.

D. CRITICISMS FROM WITHIN THE MOVEMENT

1. *Where stress is placed upon entire sanctification, there is a corresponding stress upon individual responsibility and piety, which sometimes results in individualism and divisions.* It is easy for a critical spirit to enter, and for one to become judgmental of fellow Christians.

Christian perfection is an individual matter but it must not be self-centered. A corrective to this would be to lay greater stress upon the term *katartidzō,* which means "corporate perfection." It would be well also to notice passages in the New Testament in which perfect love is linked with unity of the Spirit (Eph. 4:1-16). It cannot be too strongly stressed that to be well pleasing to God means to be in harmony with God's other children. John tells us that if we love God, we must love the brethren also (1 John 4:21). This love works no ill to his neighbor but is the fulfilling of the law (Rom. 13:10).

2. *A criticism often heard in recent years is that both the early Methodists and modern evangelicals have little social concern.* Of the early Methodists this was certainly not true. John Wesley was eager, not only to pluck brands from the burning, but also to extinguish the fire. He was not only interested in relieving by handouts the immediate needs of the poor, but also in eliminating the causes of poverty. He was equally interested in prison reform, in prohibition of the slave trade, and in promoting temperance. As noted elsewhere, the early Methodists were exceptionally zealous in social service.

Because of our emphasis on individual perfection, modern evangelicals have often shown too little concern with corporate evils and their relief. Many of us have been otherworldly; we think that time spent on making this world better is wasted effort. The scriptural position, however, is to work, to wait, to watch, and to pray. We are to wait, not in idleness but in diligence; seeking, on the one hand, to make the present

84

generation better, and on the other hand, to prepare ourselves to meet the Lord.

3. *It has been said that stress on the second crisis tends to minimize process and growth.* This is probably true, if not in theory, at least in practice. No doubt the struggle to emphasize a disputed theological point has led to the stress upon crisis. Because process has not been disputed, there has been less attention paid to it. Where there is imbalance, it can be rectified by giving greater attention to the process. Sangster's stress upon a moment-by-moment experience in grace is wholesome, scriptural, and needed now.

The early Methodists questioned among themselves whether the stress upon a crisis tended to make them minimize the fact that every moment they were either displeasing or pleasing to God by their actions, words, and attitudes. To recognize this danger and to guard against it is half the battle in overcoming it. We need to stress the crisis with clarity, and we need a corresponding stress upon process and growth in grace.

The term *eradication* linked with the crisis experience is not a bad term, even though unscriptural, provided it is used as one of several analogies and not as a definition. The term has the advantage of emphasizing the difference between the source of sin and its effect. The disadvantage lies in making sin appear to be materialistic. If the figure is used, other analogies should be used along with this one.

The analogy of light and darkness is helpful in stressing how one who has been cleansed can become infected again. The way to get rid of darkness is to turn on the light; as light comes in, the darkness goes. So as the Holy Spirit comes into the human life, sin is expelled.

Another analogy is that of fever in the body. When infection occurs, the healthy corpuscles try to seal off the infected portion, and in the struggle sometimes the temperature rises and blood poisoning may result. If the contest is successful and the health-giving corpuscles are victorious, health is restored. If resistance becomes lower, however, reinfection may occur at a later time. In a parallel experience, temptations may overpower one who is neglectful of the means of grace.

4. *It has been said that experience-centered teaching tends*

to be subjective and minimizes the centrality of Christ. It is true that sometimes those of this tradition have stressed their own perfection more than the power of Christ. While this was not true of Wesley, it is true of some of his spiritual descendants; but it need not be so. The more holy we are, the more Christlike we will be. It is the function of the Holy Spirit to take the things of Christ and show them to us. Jesus said of the Spirit that He would not speak of himself, but "he shall take the things of Christ and reveal them." The Spirit-filled person, then, looks away from himself to his Lord and seeks, as his supreme desire, to be more like Jesus.

E. Summary

What is the influence of this doctrine on the life of the individual adherent? Is it true that there is not much difference in the way our theology works out in actual life? Is it true that those who are in earnest about pleasing God, whether in the Arminian or the Reformed tradition, are very similar? We grant that the difference may be more in theory than in practice; more in theology than in life.

The greater hesitancy to testify to deliverance from sin in this life on the part of the Calvinists is due in part to their more inclusive definition of sin. It is not usually a plea for remaining in sin. It is not fair to say that everyone who opposes this doctrine does so because he wants to defend sin.

By and large, however, those who seek to be filled with the Spirit tend to be more disciplined in their daily living than others who may be equally evangelical but who do not stress the Spirit-filled life.

Is it true that all anger is sinful, as some evangelicals insist? Is it not true that Jesus looked about upon the Pharisees "with anger, grieved at their hardness of heart"? (Mark 3:5, RSV). What does Paul mean in his admonition to "be angry but do not sin; do not let the sun go down on your anger"? (Eph. 4:26, RSV). Is it possible for a sanctified Christian to be in the presence of evil and not to be indignantly opposed? Can one really love holiness without hating sin?

The essential criteria as to whether or not anger is righteous is whether it is unselfishly motivated. Selfish anger is sinful;

anger that is not sinful is anger in which self does not stand to benefit personally. As Paul exemplifies in Gal. 5:12, anger may be righteous when a just cause is involved, when justice is jeopardized, when basic doctrines or principles are imperiled.

Why is it that after one seeks and finds purity of heart and the infilling of the Spirit, there often come times when impatience erupts into anger, when there are temptations to pride and self-sufficiency, when the witness of the Spirit grows dim or nonexistent? Why do these experiences keep recurring? Why is it that so few have an uninterrupted life of victory while they are in the spiritual land of Canaan?

Pastor Harry A. Ironside experienced this, observed it in others, and decided that the theory was wrong. Others have experienced this but decided that the theory was right and that they were wrong. It is probably true that many who sincerely believe that they have the experience of perfect love do not in fact always possess it. It is also true that some go on professing it after they have lost it. But it is better to blame oneself than to reject a doctrine that has such solid scriptural and historical basis.

The one who has experienced full salvation knows the way to enter it again. Do we not need to pray, "Forgive us our trespasses," and "Lead us not into temptation"? Should there not be among us a greater readiness to admit our shortcomings and to make apologies when occasion warrants? In our tradition it is commendable when a sinner confesses his sin. Should it not also be acceptable among us if saints confess their failures when they need to do so?

How can one lose the experience of perfect love unconsciously? This may be analogous to Samson who knew not when the Spirit of God departed from him. One can lose his experience of saving grace in the same way and not realize it until there is an awakening, until his Lord appears, saying, "I have somewhat against thee. . . . repent, and do the first works." The best safeguard against failure is a daily discipline of prayer, searching of the heart, reading the Scripture, and walking in the light.

What is the best term to define deliverance from indwelling sin? If *eradication* is not the best word, what is better? William E. Sangster preferred the phrase *perfect in love*. This seems to have been a favorite with Wesley as well. There is a lack of precision, in Wesley and in most of his followers; we use *sanctification* when *entire sanctification* is meant. We should remember that those in the Reformed tradition, who do not believe in entire sanctification, frequently use the term *sanctified*. We need to remind ourselves that in this sense all Christians are sanctified. If we mean something more than this, we should use the term *entirely sanctified*. Such phrases as *the deeper life* may avoid giving offense but also may not provide much stimulus. They are not to be excluded, but they are not very definitive.

Chapter 8

The Holiness Message
and Contemporary Issues

A. SOCIAL CONCERNS

1. Social Action

In the New Testament, as in the Old, there is seldom a mention of the importance of loving God without including also, in the same breath, loving one's neighbor as oneself. This means a concern, not only for the neighbor's eternal welfare, but also for his temporal well-being. The early Methodists, illuminated and motivated by the Spirit of God, adopted similar attitudes and practices at a time when social consciousness was not well developed. They sought prison reforms in the 18th century when penal institutions were devoid of justice and mercy, and failed to rehabilitate the criminal.

Frugality and greater prosperity were by-products of the evangelical awakening as well as of the industrial revolution. The effects of this teaching on Christian stewardship are to be seen today throughout the world. Recently on "The Lutheran Hour," a sermon warned against the misuse of money and against the delusion that money, and what it can buy, is one of the most important things in life. Wesley's sermon on the use of money was a pioneer in the field.[1]

In his sermon Wesley urged that we earn all we can without hurting ourselves or our neighbor. He next urged that we save all we can, that we be frugal and disciplined in our use of money.

---

1. Wesley, "The Use of Money," *Sermons* (preached first in 1744).

He would have nothing spent for self-indulgence, gratification of the appetites, merely "keeping up with the Joneses," or pampering children with useless gadgets. He rather èxhorts to be good stewards and to give all we can to the work of God. This admonition was not against the use of money but against its misuse. To this end Wesley urged simplicity as well as neatness in appearance. Wesley's views are perhaps even more relevant now than in his own day because wealth has increased and because secularism is an increasingly accepted way of life.

2. Natural Science

Wesley was also quick to recognize and exploit science in the relief of human suffering. He set up, for example, a public clinic in which he had installed a "medical machine," a pioneering attempt to bring relief to the people. Few men knew better than did Wesley the ills of the society in which he lived and labored. The Hulsean lecturer for 1895 said, "The man who did most to reform the social life of England in the last century was John Wesley. His appeal was direct; it was an appeal to the individual; his aim was to reach the heart and conscience of each man."[2] Wesley was clear and emphatic in urging his followers to refrain from slovenliness, laziness, filthiness, tobacco, snuff, and alcohol. He was especially stern with drunkards. He appealed to the smugglers to change their occupation.

Wesley preached as well as practiced visiting the poor, relieving the sick, attending to the orphans and widows. Samuel Johnson complained that he could not get Wesley to engage in conversation for more than an hour before he had to run off to help some poor person. The indirect results of the Evangelical Revival included the formation of the British and Foreign Bible Society, the Religious Tract Society, the London Missionary Society; even the Church Missionary Society owes much to his impetus.

Wesley would have only contempt for a science that disregarded human welfare or sought to undermine the bases for faith. He distrusted the boasted achievements of human reason apart from divine revelation.

2. D. D. Thompson, *John Wesley as a Social Reformer* (New York: Eaton and Mains, 1898), p. 24.

3. Civil Liberties

Wesley was concerned with the rights of the individual, with civil rights. On February 12, 1772, he joined in the denunciation of slavery as "that execrable sum of all villainies." His most powerful contribution to the antislavery movement was his *Thoughts on Slavery,* a pamphlet of 53 pages published in 1774. "No more severe arraignment of slavery was ever written."[3] Some regard it as influential as was *Uncle Tom's Cabin* later in arousing popular condemnation for the slave trade. The last letter that Wesley wrote, only four days before his death, was upon the subject of slavery. It was addressed to William Wilberforce, the leader of the movement for the emanicipation of slaves in the West Indies. In it Wesley characterized American slavery as "the vilest that ever saw the sun." Wilberforce was addressed as "an Athanasius *contra mundum";* Wesley urged him to "go on in the name of God."

John Wesley abhorred the institution of slavery. His evangelical contemporary George Whitefield not only approved it but became a slaveholder. At the time of his death, he owned 75 slaves on his orphanage house plantations. Whitefield tended to justify this by the necessity of relieving the white people of drudgery and adding to their prosperity. He also justified it on the basis that it might provide an opportunity to preach the gospel and give to the Negroes a hope of life everlasting. This, he said, "swallows up all temporal inconveniences whatsoever."[4]

The modern holiness movement appears to have been more in the tradition of Whitefield than of Wesley with reference to its attitude toward slavery and civil rights. With the exception of a few feeble protests, the modern holiness movement and contemporary evangelists have until recently been relatively indifferent to the needs of minorities and their civil rights.

There are notable exceptions. Asa Mahan, of Oberlin College, was deeply influenced by Wesleyan theology and urged abolition of slavery. The Wesleyan Methodist church originated in western New York on the issue of abolition. After the Civil

---

3. *Ibid.,* p. 47.
4. George Whitefield, "Letter to John Wesley from Bristol," March 22, 1751, *Works* (London: E. and C. Dilly, 1771).

War this concern for social justice gave way to a concern for purity of life and of faith.

If Wesley were here today, he would be articulate in demanding that love for one's neighbor express itself in invitations to fellowship and to worship on a common basis. He would call for the abolition of discrimination in employment, in housing, in education, and in public accommodations. He would be calling for equality of opportunity without respect to ancestral origin. Because he was a conservative with great respect for law and order, it is questionable whether he would approve civil rights demonstrations, even to support good causes. But he would be an eloquent and articulate social justice witness, whether in sermon or editorial or possibly in a march. He would doubtless urge his preachers by precept and example, to make it clear that no one on the basis of race should be excluded from their congregations, or homes, or fellowship.

4. War and Peace

Wesley spoke indignantly at the spectacle of the kings of England and France trying to settle their differences by going to war and men dying as a result. Would he today be a "hawk," a "dove," or an "owl"?

Donald and Lucille Dayton conclude that "Wesley himself seems not to have struggled deeply with this question."[5] In his essay on "Original Sin," however, Wesley denounced war in the strongest terms; for him, it illustrated the effect of original sin. He asks, "Who can reconcile war, I will not say to religious, but, to any degree of reason or common sense?"

Nevertheless, in 1745, at a time of internal military crisis, Wesley was more concerned with swearing among the soldiers than about the issues of war or peace. He was a loyalist, supportive of the king, but kept warning that the best weapon for defense was the fear of God. Wesley wrote to the mayor and to the general that his own finest contribution in the common defense would be to preach to the soldiers, "to call these poor

5. Donald and Lucille Dayton, "An Historical Survey of Attitudes Toward War and Peace Within the American Holiness Movement," 1973 (unpublished), p. 2.

sinners to repentance."[6] Thus Wesley set a precedent for military chaplains.

At the first and most influential Methodist conference, in 1745, it was agreed that it was lawful to bear arms, because it is not forbidden in the New Testament and because Cornelius the centurion was not condemned for his militarism. Later, in 1782, Wesley was more concerned with the breaking of the Sabbath by the soldiers than with the military establishment as such. John Fletcher wrote that "so long as the wicked shall use the sword in support of vice, the righteous who are in power, must use it in defense of virtue."[7] With reference to the American Revolution, Fletcher concluded that "the most bloody civil war is preferable to the horrible consequences of daring anarchy." Richard Watson, in more temperate language, considered war compatible with Christianity only as a "last resort," as a means of assuring commercial prosperity and national independence. He felt, however, that Christianity tended to make war less brutal.

Among American Methodists, the attitude of Francis Asbury was ambiguous; but Jesse Lee concluded that he could kill none of his "fellow creatures." Freeborn Garretson, another itinerant preacher, renounced warfare as did Philip Gatch, both taking a noncombatant role amid much persecution. Thus the pacifist stance was more pronounced among American Methodists than in the parent body in Britain.

This difference of emphasis within the Wesleyan tradition continued through the 19th century but intensified, both as a result of the Civil War and also because of an increasing emphasis on the doctrine of entire sanctification. The latter resulted in the American holiness movement which germinated within Methodism but was not confined therein; the movement consistently sought to be supradenominational. The more conservative phase of the movement increased in influence from 1830 on and remained within the older and larger denominations. The more radical phase led by "separatists" left the parent churches and formed several small denominations, the Wesleyans and Free Methodists being the first. The Wesleyans

6. Letter to Mr. Ridley, mayor of Newcastle. Luke Tyerman, *Life and Times of John Wesley* (London: Sangster, 1878), 1:494.
7. Dayton, "War and Peace," p. 3.

originated in 1843 with abolition as the main issue. They were emphatic in renunciation of "war in all its forms." By 1847 and 1848 two Wesleyan conferences had made the refusal to engage in war, as well as renouncing slavery, the condition for membership.[8]

The Wesleyans and Free Methodists, like the early Methodists, committed themselves to the twofold task of "reforming the nation and spreading scriptural holiness." Many holiness leaders, including Asa Mahan, strongly denounced the war with Mexico (1846-48). Later, however, when the Civil War became imminent, they strongly supported the Northern cause. Abolitionist sentiments were now separated from pacifism. The American Peace Society, the Wesleyans, Asa Mahan, John Inskip, and other leaders in the holiness movement strongly supported the Northern cause. The author of the "Battle Hymn of the Republic" doubtless felt her convictions had their source in the Scriptures.

After the Civil War, three movements—revivalism, the emphasis on holy living, and the peace groups—tended to coalesce. But the emphasis shifted from the "reformation of manners" to cultivation of the inner life. Two reasons may be given for what the Daytons term the "consistent erosion of the earlier concerns for peace" among churches in the Wesleyan tradition. One cited by them is the increasing conformity to the dominant cultural patterns of society. The other reason was the emergence of ruthless Fascism, Nazism, and Communism. The latter was particularly dangerous because of its commitment to domination of the world by force as well as by indoctrination. The majority in the Methodist tradition have felt that wars of aggression are unjust but not wars in self-defense or assistance in the self-defense of other nations.

The issue remains one of the most pressing and persistent for sensitive Christians who seek to be complete in their commitment to Christ and at the same time relevant in their world. Most of them find nonresistance a personal option but not an option for society as a whole. They conclude that evil-doers must be restrained by force as a last resort when no other options are available to protect the innocent.

8. *Ibid.*, p. 7.

5. Capital Punishment

The Wesleys rode with a condemned man to the gallows; today they might discourage capital punishment in the hope that time would help the soul to find the Saviour.

B. RELIGIOUS CONCERNS

1. The Ecumenical Movement

As an evangelical seeking to live according to the New Testament, Wesley could be as uncompromising as Paul in matters of doctrine. For this reason he split with the Moravians on the issue of the means of grace. At the same time, he is the author of a sermon entitled "On Having a Catholic Spirit." In it he said differences of opinion would not keep him from having fellowship with others who were likeminded with himself. Today he would doubtless be prominent in the ecumenical movement, urging unity if not union—but unity on the basis of Christ and not simply for union as an end in itself. He would be alert to the importance of unity in order to make witnessing effective.

Because Wesley was in the Pietist tradition, which places emphasis on transformed living, he would feel at home among others likeminded in their love for Christ, notwithstanding differences of background. Latitude in the area of opinions, unity in doctrinal essentials, and liberty in church polity are the essential ingredients in a true ecumenicity greatly needed today. Wesley would have little sympathy with splinter groups who separate in order to preserve their own vested interests or leadership opportunities. He would have scant sympathy for a parochial point of view that considers self-preservation more important than evangelical witness to the world. He would certainly rebuke predatory "evangelism" in which some groups grow by feeding on sister churches. In this area it is important to do unto others as we would have others do unto us; and at the same time to seek, in the unity of the Spirit, the "measure of the stature of the fulness of Christ."

Areas of fruitful cooperation today include wholesome recreation such as a neighborhood project between Catholic and Protestant churches. In education, evangelicals (i.e., Protestants who are conservative in theology) cooperate effectively in Bible institutes (in Colombia), in colleges, and on the seminary level (e.g., in Yeotmal, India; Wilmore, Ky.; and Medellin, Colombia): also in publications in Bangarapet, India (WGM), Bible Meditation League, Pocket Testament League, Wesleyans in Colombia; in the Aldersgate Publications Association (Free Methodists, Nazarenes, Wesleyans, and others), and especially in social action (World Vision, etc.). Now, when Christianity is confronted with paganism, indifference, and evangelistic Marxism, united action is imperative. Jesus prayed "that they all may be one; . . . that the world may believe" (John 17:21). This is to be achieved, not by erasing theological distinctions but by Christian fellowship *(koinonia)*.

2. Theological Trends

Neoorthodoxy successfully challenged 19th-century theological liberalism by denying the inherent goodness of human nature and man's capacity to improve himself or to "bring in the kingdom." Neoorthodoxy also insisted on the necessity of divine initiative in grace and on recovering the Reformation principle of justification by faith alone. But neoorthodoxy was deficient in its doctrine of grace, in its views of the accuracy of the Bible, and in its Barthian advocacy of the "ontological impossibility of sin," with its corollary of universalism.[9]

In his *Römerbrief,* Barth argues that Romans 7 (more than chapter 8) is the best the gospel can do, i.e., make us aware of our sinfulness. Chapter 8, however, expresses Paul's joyous announcement of deliverance. There is in neoorthodoxy some of the antinomianism that one finds in Reformation theology.[10]

---

9. Karl Barth, *Church Dogmatics,* p. 353 (cited in Herbert Hartwell, *The Theology of Karl Barth* [Philadelphia: Westminster Press, 1964], p. 174): "To quote Barth's own definition of grace: 'grace is the inner being and self-conduct of God which distinguishes His doing directed towards the seeking and creating of fellowship by the fact that it is determined by His own free inclination, favour and benevolence, unconditioned by an unworthiness or opposition in the latter—able, on the contrary, to overcome all unworthiness and opposition.'"

10. *Ibid.,* p. 84. "With Barth divine grace is not an abstract or general principle, not 'a supernatural something in man coming forth from God' (Aquinas) . . . transmitted to man 'as a permanent gift of sanctifying power'" (Hartwell, p. 168). God's grace is "His presence in His Word, in all His actions and works" (p. 169). Grace is God's personal presence rather than a gift bestowed by God upon man. Barth rejected the Roman Catholic distinction between God's grace *(gratia increata)* and "the grace received and possessed by man *(gratia creata)*" (Barth, CD, p. 84).

Dialectical theology owes much to the philosophy of Immanuel Kant. It has no place or sympathy for what Reinhold Niebuhr deprecates as "pretentions to perfection."

3. Existentialism

As World War I contributed to the rise of a dialectical "theology of tension," so World War II witnessed the dominance of existentialism led by the philosophy of atheist Martin Heiddiger and the theology of Rudolph Bultmann. In this philosophy, being is deemed more essential than knowing, existence more important than essence. Commendable is Bultmann's avowed purpose of interpreting the gospel in terms convincing to modern man. His emphasis on decision is also congenial to evangelical theologians.

Bultmann, however, thinks it possible to have "the Easter faith" without the Easter fact. Existentialism is too subjective; it finds little importance in the historical Jesus. A faith which lacks objective basis in fact is like a bouquet of flowers which, cut off from their roots, will soon wither and die. Barth once described existentialism as like old-fashioned liberalism revived. It makes little use of either historical research or reason, relying instead on subjective criteria. It is worse than either liberalism or neoorthodoxy. Wesleyan theology knew the importance of confrontation and decision decades before the advent of existentialism.

Today Bultmann and the existentialists are being challenged and replaced by a new "quest for the historical Jesus" led by men like Pannenberg in Germany and James M. Robinson in the United States. Thus today's theologians are returning to the quest for the historical Jesus undertaken by the late Albert Schweitzer more than a half century ago.

4. Liberation Theology

In the 1970s "the theology of liberation" is a focus of attention, especially in Europe and Latin America. Frederick Herzog of Duke Divinity School insists that biblical theology is linked with Protestantism and with affluence. It therefore tends to defend the upper classes and the status quo. He points out that the Bible presents God and the incarnate Jesus as concerned with the poor. Therefore unless the interpreter of

Scripture identifies with today's poor and oppressed, he cannot even understand the Bible.[11] "Liberation theology" suspects that self-styled "scientific exegesis" is irrelevant to the urgent social-political-economic issues of today.

In Latin America there is developing a polarization between conservative Catholic theologians who are eager to keep the status quo and Catholic theologians of liberation who warn that the predicament of the underprivileged can no longer be ignored. Liberation theologians point to God's redemptive acts in history as actions of liberation of the poor, especially in the Exodus and in the creation of a nation under a covenant which guaranteed equality of opportunity for all. Liberation theology demands that orthodoxy now become orthopraxy—that doctrine be followed by deeds. Gutiérrez sees three levels of liberation: political, historical, and liberation from sin.[12]

A chief spokesman for "black theology" cites the biblical emphasis on the deliverance from Egypt and the prophetic condemnation of oppressions. He sees these as mandates for the church today to champion the cause of the poor of the earth. Indeed he points out that any theology which does not concern itself with the underprivileged is not authentically Christian.[13]

For those in the Wesleyan tradition this "theology of liberation" is a reminder that historically the evangelicals not only preached to the poor but also served them. When the Wesleyan message is beamed primarily to the middle classes, it ceases to that extent from being truly Christian. To neglect the underprivileged is to deny Christ. To be concerned only with those in a position to give economic support to the church is a betrayal of the Christian gospel.

5. Relational Theology

In recent years there are voices heard in the holiness movement that articulate what is termed a "theology of relationship." It is correctly pointed out that all relationships, both

11. Frederick Herzog, "Liberation Hermeneutic and Ideology Critique," *Interpretation* (October, 1974), pp. 387-403.

12. Gustavo Gutiérrez, *A Theology of Liberation* (Mary Knoll, N.Y.: Orbis Books, 1973), pp. 149-87.

13. James H. Cone, "Biblical Revelation and Social Existence," *Interpretation* (October, 1974), pp. 429, 437.

the divine-human and interpersonal relations, are conceived in dynamic rather than in static terms. In this context process is stressed more than crisis; the relational is set over against the substantial.[14] It is also charged that many in the holiness movement favor crisis and minimize process, that sin is regarded as substantial rather than as spiritual in nature.

There are some in holiness ranks who assert that Wesley and the Scripture stand against these recent self-styled "Wesleyan" voices; they believe that the relational advocates need to be realigned with the biblical-Wesleyan positions.

The writer sees this emphasis on relational theology as a valid one. Life itself is dynamic rather than static. In the Bible the idea of covenant is a relationship that is all-pervasive. But wherein is the emphasis unique enough to merit a new label? Is there anything in the divine-human encounter that is not one of relationship? In the Scriptures God is related to man as Father, but He also is envisioned as Judge, King, Husband, and Shepherd—all of which involve relationships.

It is true, however, that care needs to be taken not to stress crisis to the neglect of process, or "states of grace" to the neglect of growth in grace. This peril was recognized in the earliest Methodist conferences, yet John Wesley in his later days stressed the crisis aspect. This stress was given probably because the crisis was a neglected emphasis rather than because it was more important than growth in holiness.

Asa Mahan, Phoebe Palmer, Thomas Upham, and others in the modern holiness movement, as well as the Keswick conferences and Pentecostalism, have also stressed a second crisis because it has been neglected elsewhere, not because it was more important. As often happens when stressing a point that others deny or neglect, holiness preachers may have taken growth for granted and hence neglected it.

Some relational theologians object to the use of substantive terms. Methodist theologian Mudge once advised not to use such terms as "new birth" but rather a "rectification of the will" to describe conversion. However, concrete terms and pictorial language are widely used in Scripture with no impairment to effective communication. Many claim to have seen the

14. Mildred Bangs Wynkoop, *A Theology of Love* (Kansas City: Beacon Hill Press of Kansas City, 1972), p. 105, *passim*.

sun "rise"—a pictorial way of describing the phenomenon—
without endorsing the Ptolemaic theory that the sun goes
around the earth each day. As long as the language of Scripture
continues to be used, such biblical figures of speech as "blood,"
"heart," "put off," and "put on," will probably continue to
convey spiritual rather than crudely literal meanings. Who does
not believe in relational theology?

C. Summary

The data of Scripture seems decisive in support of Wesley's
broad interpretation and emphasis. Said Wesley, "Let God be
true, but every man a liar." Man cannot veto the Word of God.
It should be remembered—that there is no doctrinal movement
exempt from injury by both friends and enemies. Nor is a
doctrine safe from deviations on the part of its advocates. The
doctrine of perfect love has perhaps had no more than its share
of such misrepresentation.

A New Wesleyanism has been called for. Does someone
need to revitalize the emphases of the Evangelical Revival as
Barth did for Lutheranism and Calvinism? Perhaps the best
way to achieve this goal would be to release a new movement
in evangelism with theology as a secondary consideration.

It is encouraging to note in the decade of the 70s a trend in
the direction of evangelical Christianity. *Time* and *U.S. News
and World Report* (June 4, 1973) are among observers who see
theological liberalism declining in influence and conservative
churches and schools growing. This is attested also in Dean
Kelley, *Why Conservative Churches Are Growing.*

Interest in the doctrine and experience of entire sanctification seems to have been more pronounced in English-speaking
countries a century ago than it is today. That was probably
due to the influence of the Second Great Awakening in America,
to the revivals led by Charles Finney, perhaps to the novelty
of the doctrine, and to the Moody-Sankey revivals. When there
is a new generation of converts, there is a new interest in
purity and power for witnessing.

Today the revival campaigns of the Graham evangelistic
teams, Campus Crusade, and other organizations with an
emphasis upon regeneration and renewal may stimulate a new

surge of interest in the deeper life. As this occurs, we shall witness a renewed thrust of the holiness movement.

Let us hope, also, that Pentecostalism will come to a more scriptural and orthodox position. Let us pray that the Jesus Movement will mature into a theologically articulate and spiritually dynamic element in the Christian Church. Above all, let us keep our eyes upon Christ and follow Him step by step. Let us see ourselves not so much as custodians of a glorious heritage, but rather as individuals who seek, find, affirm, and thus perpetuate the life of scriptural holiness.

> *He wills that I should holy be,*
>   *That holiness I long to feel;*
> *That full divine conformity*
>   *To all my Saviour's righteous will.*
>
> *No more I stagger at Thy pow'r,*
>   *Or doubt Thy truth, which cannot move;*
> *Hasten the long expected hour,*
>   *And bless me with Thy perfect love.*
>
> —CHARLES WESLEY

Bibliography

Agnew, Milton S. *Transformed Christians.* Kansas City: Beacon Hill Press of Kansas City, 1974.

Barth, Karl. *Church Dogmatics.* Translated by G. T. Thomson. New York: Charles Scribner's Sons, 1955.

Bauer, Walter E. "The Philosophy of the American Revolution," *God and Ceasar.* Edited by W. A. Quanbeck. Minneapolis: Augsburg Publishing House, 1959.

Brown, C. E. *The Meaning of Sanctification.* Anderson, Ind.: Warner Press, 1945.

Bruner, F. D. *A Theology of the Holy Spirit*. Grand Rapids, Mich.: Wm. B. Eerdmans Publishing Co., 1970.

Burtner, R. W., and Chiles, R. E., eds. *A Compend of Wesley's Theology*. Nashville: Abingdon Press, 1954.

Cannon, W. R. *The Theology of John Wesley*. New York: Abingdon-Cokesbury Press, 1946.

Carter, C. W. *The Person and Ministry of the Holy Spirit*. Grand Rapids, Mich.: Baker Book House, 1974.

Cattell, Everett L. *The Spirit of Holiness*. Grand Rapids, Mich.: Wm. B. Eerdmans Publishing Co., 1968.

Cone, James H. "Biblical Revelation and Social Existence." *Interpretation*, October, 1974.

Cox, Leo G. *John Wesley's Concept of Perfection*. Kansas City: Beacon Hill Press, 1964.

Dayton, Donald and Lucille. "An Historical Survey of Attitudes Toward War and Peace Within the American Holiness Movement." (Unpublished bibliographical essay).

Deschner, John. *Wesley's Christology*. Dallas: Southern Methodist Press, 1969.

Duewel, Wesley L. *The Holy Spirit and Tongues*. Winona Lake, Ind.: Light and Life Press, 1974.

Dunn, J. D. G. *Baptism in the Holy Spirit*. Naperville, Ill.: Allenson, 1970.

Earle, Ralph. *Word Meanings in the New Testament*. Kansas City, Mo.: Beacon Hill Press of Kansas City, 1974.

Erdman, C. R. *The Spirit of Christ*. New York: R. Smith, 1929.

Gaster, T. H. (translator). *The Dead Sea Scriptures*. New York: Doubleday and Co., 1964.

Geiger, Kenneth, ed. *Further Insights into Holiness*. Kansas City: Beacon Hill Press, 1963.

Gutiérrez, Gustavo. *A Theology of Liberation*. Mary Knoll, N.Y.: Orbis Books, 1973.

Hartwell, Herbert. *The Theology of Karl Barth*. Philadelphia: Westminster Press, 1964.

Hayes, J. H. *A Political and Cultural History of Modern Europe*. New York: The Macmillan Co., 1936.

Hendry, George S. *The Holy Spirit in Christian Theology*. Philadelphia: Westminster Press, 1954.

Herzog, Frederick. "Liberation Hermeneutic and Ideology Critique." *Interpretation*, October, 1974.

Hildebrandt, F. *Christianity According to the Wesleys*. London: Epworth Press, 1956.

Hollenweger, W. J. *The Pentecostals*. Translated by R. A. Wilson. Minneapolis: Augsburg Press, 1972.

Hostetler, Paul, ed. *Perfect Love and War.* Nappanee, Ind.: Evangel Press, 1974.

Howard, Richard E. *Newness of Life.* Kansas City: Beacon Hill Press of Kansas City, 1975.

Hulme, W. E. *The Dynamics of Sanctification.* Minneapolis: Augsburg Press, 1966.

James, Maynard. *I Believe in the Holy Ghost.* Minneapolis: Bethany Fellowship, Inc., 1965.

Lake, K., ed. *Apostolic Fathers.* New York: G. P. Putnam's Sons, 1930.

Lietzman, Hans. *Beginnings of the Christian Church.* New York: Charles Scribner's Sons, 1937.

Mavis, W. C. *The Psychology of Christian Experience.* Grand Rapids, Mich.: Zondervan Publishing House, 1963.

McGiffert, A. C. *Protestant Thought Before Kant.* New York: Charles Scribner's Sons, 1933.

Meyer, F. B. "The Filling of The Holy Spirit" in *The Power of Pentecost.* Edited by T. Waugh. Chicago: Moody Press, n.d.

Mullins, E. Y. "Baptism of the Holy Spirit," *The International Standard Bible Encyclopaedia.* 5 vols. Chicago: Howard-Severance Co., 1930.

Murray, Andrew. *The Holiest of All.* Old Tappan, N.J.: Fleming H. Revell Co., 1962.

Neill, Stephen. *Christian Holiness.* London: Lutterworth Press, 1960.

Parr, F. O. *Perfect Love and Race Hatred.* Bourbonnais, Ill.: (Privately published), 1964.

Parris, John R. *Wesley's Doctrine of the Sacraments.* London: Epworth Press, 1963.

Purkiser, W. T. *Sanctification and Its Synonyms.* Kansas City: Beacon Hill Press, 1962.

———. *The Gifts of the Spirit.* Kansas City: Beacon Hill Press of Kansas City, 1975.

Sangster, W. E. *The Path to Perfection.* New York: Abingdon Press, 1943.

Smith, Timothy. *Revivalism and Social Reform.* Nashville: Abingdon Press, 1957.

Snaith, N. P. *The Distinctive Ideas of the Old Testament.* London: Epworth Press, 1944.

Starkey, L. M. *The Work of the Holy Spirit: A Study in Wesleyan Theology.* New York: Abingdon Press, 1962.

Stott, J. R. W. *The Baptism and Fullness of the Holy Spirit.* Downers Grove, Ill.: Inter-Varsity Press, 1964, 1971.

Taylor, R. S. *A Right Conception of Sin.* Kansas City: Beacon Hill Press, 1945.

Thompson, D. D. *John Wesley as a Social Reformer*. New York: Eaton and Mains, 1898.

Turner, George A. *The Vision Which Transforms*. Kansas City: Beacon Hill Press, 1964.

Tyerman, Luke. *Life and Times of John Wesley*. London: James Sangster, 1876.

Unger, M. F. "The Baptism with the Holy Spirit." *Bibliotheca Sacra*, Dallas Theological Seminary, CI, Nos. 402-3, April-September, 1944.

Waugh, Thomas, ed. *The Power of Pentecost*. Chicago: Moody Press, n.d.

Wesley, John. *A Plain Account of Christian Perfection*. Kansas City: Beacon Hill Press of Kansas City, 1968.

———. *Explanatory Notes upon the New Testament*. London: The Epworth Press, 1941.

———. *Journal*. Edited by N. Curnock. London: Epworth Press, 1909-16.

———. *Sermons*. 3rd American ed. Edited by John Emory. 2 vols. New York: Eaton and Mains, 1825.

———. *The Letters of John Wesley*. Edited by John Telford. 8 vols. London: Epworth Press, 1931.

———. *Wesley's Standard Sermons*. Edited by Edward H. Sugden. 2 vols. London: Epworth Press, 1921.

———. *Works*. 3rd ed. Edited by T. Jackson. 14 vols. London: Wesleyan-Methodist Book Room, 1929-31.

Whitefield, George. *Works*. London: E. R. C. Dilly, 1771.

Williams, Colin. *John Wesley's Theology Today*. New York: Abingdon Press, 1960.

Wood, I. F. *The Spirit of God in Biblical Literature*. New York: A. C. Armstrong and Son, 1904.

Wood, Skevington. *John Wesley, The Burning Heart*. Grand Rapids, Mich.: Wm. B. Eerdmans Publishing Co., 1967.

Wynkoop, Mildred Bangs. *A Theology of Love*. Kansas City: Beacon Hill Press of Kansas City, 1972.

———. *John Wesley, Christian Revolutionary*. Kansas City: Beacon Hill Press of Kansas City, 1970.